"The dynamic duo of Growe and Sturdevant has written a true, must-read historical narrative that is also an intimate story of 'one of our League's own.' More importantly, they've captured the essence of Joan's life message for us all: change is always possible, *but only if we turn out*—to vote, to learn, to advocate—as active participants in our democracy."

> —Michelle Swarmer Witte, executive director,
> League of Women Voters Minnesota

"Minnesota's iconic former secretary of state, Joan Growe, has written a timely book about her work to promote transparency in government and protect one of our most fundamental freedoms, our sovereign right as citizens to speak and be heard—our right to vote. It is an inspiring must-read for anyone who values this right and wishes to learn how best to preserve it."

> —Paul Anderson, former associate justice,
> Minnesota Supreme Court

"Having served six terms as secretary of state, Joan Growe is a Minnesota treasure. She was first elected when women were just beginning to enter politics, and her stories of challenges and accomplishments will engage and inspire a new generation of leaders. Readers will especially benefit from Growe's expertise on election reform and her insights on reducing barriers to voting, reforming election administration, and increasing government accountability."

> —Kathryn Pearson, associate professor of political science,
> University of Minnesota

"This remarkable book was written for all who love our democracy and who worry about how it is doing, given nonstop assaults from enemies—foreign and domestic. Joan Growe presents a treasure chest of inspiring stories and wisdom-infused warnings. This book, the next chapter in her life of public service, is what you want from a true servant leader—straight talk and knowledgeable, heartfelt advice."

> —Mark Ritchie, president, Global Minnesota,
> Minnesota secretary of state, 2007–15

"The first woman elected to a Minnesota statewide office in her own right, former secretary of state Joan Growe deserves much of the credit for Minnesota leading the nation in voter turnout in the last five presidential elections—and earning the reputation as the 'state that votes.' In this clearly written memoir, Growe makes a persuasive case for why protecting voting rights and boosting political participation matters."

—Bill Salisbury, *St. Paul Pioneer Press* capitol bureau reporter

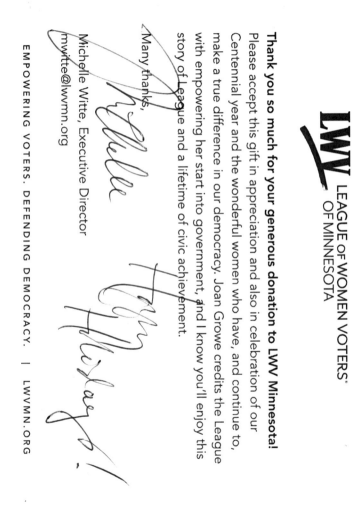

LWV LEAGUE OF WOMEN VOTERS®
OF MINNESOTA

Thank you so much for your generous donation to LWV Minnesota!
Please accept this gift in appreciation and also in celebration of our
Centennial year and the wonderful women who have, and continue to,
make a true difference in our democracy. Joan Growe credits the League
with empowering her start into government, and I know you'll enjoy this
story of League and a lifetime of civic achievement.

Many thanks,

Michelle Witte, Executive Director
mwitte@lwvmn.org

EMPOWERING VOTERS. DEFENDING DEMOCRACY. | LWVMN.ORG

TURNOUT

Making Minnesota the State That Votes

Joan Anderson Growe

with Lori Sturdevant

Foreword by Hillary Rodham Clinton

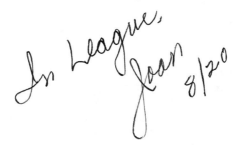

In League,
Joan 8/20

MINNESOTA
HISTORICAL
SOCIETY PRESS

CLEAN
WATER
LAND &
LEGACY
AMENDMENT

The Minnesota Historical Society Press is a member of the Association of University Presses.

Manufactured in the United States of America

10 9 8 7 6 5 4 3 2 1

∞ The paper used in this publication meets the minimum requirements of the American National Standard for Information Sciences—Permanence for Printed Library Materials, ANSI Z39.48–1984.

International Standard Book Number
ISBN: 978-1-68134-163-7 (paper)
ISBN: 978-1-68134-164-4 (e-book)

Library of Congress Cataloging-in-Publication Data

Names: Growe, Joan Anderson, author. | Sturdevant, Lori, 1953– author.
Title: Turnout : making Minnesota the state that votes / Joan Anderson Growe ; with Lori Sturdevant.
Description: Saint Paul, MN : Minnesota Historical Society Press, 2020. | Includes bibliographical references and index. | Summary: "Joan Anderson Growe, Minnesota's secretary of state from 1975 to 1999 and the architect and chief promoter of Minnesota's high voter turnout, tells her story, showing how hard work and cooperation made the state a leader in clean, open elections."—Provided by publisher.
Identifiers: LCCN 2020013679 | ISBN 9781681341637 (paperback) | ISBN 9781681341644 (ebook)
Subjects: LCSH: Voter turnout—Minnesota. | Elections—Minnesota. | Political participation—Minnesota.
Classification: LCC JK6190 .G76 2020 | DDC 324.609776—dc23
LC record available at https://lccn.loc.gov/2020013679

This and other Minnesota Historical Society Press books are available from popular e-book vendors.

For Tom
and
Sydney, Sofia, and Katie

Contents

Foreword

No one could have predicted that the hundredth anniversary of women gaining the right to vote across our country would overlap with a global pandemic that would challenge our democracy, all in a presidential election year—but here we are, and it's hard to think of a more urgent topic in America in 2020 than voting.

The right to vote is the cornerstone of our democracy. It is the muscle of our body politic. It determines whether we'll have good jobs and growing incomes, an economy that works for everyone, and access to quality, affordable health care. It influences so many facets of our lives, from the schools we attend to the roads we drive on. It powers the change we seek and the future we envision. No matter what issue you care about, the right to vote is central. And the fight to protect that fundamental right is the single greatest fight of our time. That's why we need a twenty-first-century civil rights movement devoted to claiming, enforcing, and defending the right to vote. Joan Anderson Growe has given us an excellent guide for that work— from restoring the Voting Rights Act to advocating for vote-by-mail to championing automatic voter registration and implementing laws and policies that lead to cleaner, more transparent elections.

As Joan points out, something is very wrong when millions of American citizens are systematically and deliberately kept from voting. There's a saying I first heard years ago in Arkansas: If you see a turtle sitting on a fence post, you know it didn't get there on its own. In the pages that follow, Joan traces the antidemocratic history of voter suppression from early voter registration requirements intended to deny the vote to immigrants to literacy tests and poll taxes aimed at disenfranchising African Americans to the shameful gutting of the Voting Rights Act in 2013 to present-day attempts to discourage, depress, and deter people from voting—particularly young people, the elderly, women, and people of color. She addresses the question of electoral security, demonstrating the weakness of arguments about voter fraud. She explores the damaging role of foreign interference in our elections as well as one of the biggest threats we face: the distrust, apathy, and cynicism that keep too many Americans from showing up at election time. In recent years, more people than I can count have asked me the same question: "How did we get here?" Joan's book provides an answer.

Turnout is a powerful and relevant case study in what it takes to build a voting process that's "convenient, easy, and suited to the realities of modern life." It's also a memoir of Joan's life and trailblazing career in government. In many ways, her rise through the ranks of politics mirrors the history of women's political enfranchisement in America. Joan was born just fifteen years after the Nineteenth Amendment granted women the right to vote (though it would take decades of organizing and legislation like the Voting Rights Act to secure that right for non-white women and, as Joan notes, that struggle continues today). She grew up without knowing of a single woman in any elected office on the local, state, or federal level. She made her first foray into civics through the League of Women Voters, an organization founded to continue what suffragist Carrie Chapman Catt called "a mighty political experiment" to encourage women to use their newly won electoral power. The women's movement of the 1960s opened Joan's eyes to the possibility of changing "narrow-minded attitudes about women's worth." "Almost unwittingly," she writes, "we were becoming feminists." While observing the legislative process at the state capitol, Joan came to the same realization that has inspired a new generation of women, young people, and people of color to step into the arena: "I could do better than that."

For some readers, myself included, Joan's experiences running for and serving in office will feel all too familiar. Her stories of people questioning whether a woman was "electable," or reporters asking her what it was like to run "as a woman" (as though she had another option!), are evergreen, which only underscores the work we still have to do to confront gender bias and break down barriers for women in politics and government. Joan describes one fact sheet she handed out to reporters that included helpful guidance about herself and the work of the secretary of state's office and a suggestion: "You might want to ask Joan about elections."

The lessons of Joan's grassroots, women-powered campaigns are also as essential today as ever, especially for anyone trying to break into a predominately white, male power structure. "[F]or me and the other Growe campaigners, change sprang from the encouragement we gave each other," she writes. "We saw talent in each other, and said so. We set ambitious goals and assured each other we could meet them."

At the heart of this book is a simple but powerful premise: Our democracy works best when everyone can participate, as voters and as leaders, regardless of age, race, gender, income, or ability. In the moments when progress feels slow, and the long haul seems unbearably long, the words and ideas in these pages add up to a North Star to which Minnesota and the rest of our country should aspire.

Hillary Rodham Clinton, April 2020

Introduction

The right to vote is—or ought to be—something every American holds dear. But I'll claim that my connection to that constitutionally guaranteed right is uncommonly strong. In ways both personal and professional, voting is at or near the center of my life story.

Voting in every election was an unquestioned part of the civic tradition in which I grew up. The long crusade to give American women the right to vote, which achieved its goal just fifteen years before I was born, made my career possible. The hard work of local members of the suffragists' successor organization, the League of Women Voters, put me in elective office. A desire to encourage voting motivated me every day through twenty-four years as Minnesota's secretary of state. And my concern about recent efforts to deny or discourage some citizens from voting around the nation—even in Minnesota, the state that has long led the nation in voter turnout—is among the reasons I've written this book.

This book is a memoir. But it also has a wider mission. It's my plea to my fellow Minnesotans to cherish and protect their tradition of clean, open elections. I'm convinced that the high quality of life that Minnesotans enjoy has been made possible in good measure by their habit of regular voting. When people vote in large numbers, their governments have a credibility that governments in low-voting states lack. Regular voters tend to think of government not as an alien or oppressive force but as an extension of themselves and their communities. They accept government as a useful and often uniquely effective tool for solving shared problems and achieving shared goals. They feel empowered to hold their government to account when it performs poorly. Frequent voters are more likely to see taxes not as illegitimate theft but as the rightful cost of government's work, and to understand how that work benefits them and their neighbors. As a result, society's problems are more likely to be solved.

In addition, when large numbers of people vote, political parties are less prone to being controlled by partisan zealots with extreme ideas. Those elected are beholden to true majorities, not to narrow segments of the electorate. That makes those officials more amenable to the compromises that functional representative governments require.

In the pages that follow, I describe the sound policies and practices that the Minnesota Legislature and the office of the secretary of state set in place on my watch to encourage voting. I salute the many people throughout this state whose professional or voluntary efforts have given Minnesota its reputation for excellence in election administration. And I recommend policy steps that this state and the nation might take to keep elections clean and fair and voter participation high.

This book has a decidedly feminist bent, for obvious reasons. I'm proud to have been one of the Minnesotans in the vanguard of the second-wave women's movement that swept the nation in the early 1970s. The story of that movement is inseparable from my own. I've spent a half century encouraging women to vote, join political organizations, run for office, and seek ever-larger roles in government. I'll be pleased if readers find that encouragement in this book, and delighted if they act on it.

But this book isn't intended for women alone. I hope to appeal to anyone who appreciates that women's enfranchisement was part of a larger and continuing struggle to maintain and build American democracy. Those today who seek to discourage or bar would-be voters from the polls may say that they aim only to eliminate fraud. But in state after state, the so-called remedies they've chosen would disproportionately disenfranchise the poor, people of color, and new citizens who started their lives in other countries. Meanwhile, the fraud they propose to prevent is exceedingly rare.

It will take an informed and alert citizenry to understand vote-suppression tactics as the discriminatory, antidemocratic maneuvers that they are—and to reject them. My hope is that for democracy's defenders, the story that follows both provides useful information and sounds an alarm.

January 2020

Rooted in Democracy

I t's almost as expected as snow in November. If there's a national election, a larger share of eligible voters will cast ballots in Minnesota than in any other state. By 2019, newspaper headlines announcing that Minnesota led the nation in turnout had appeared after eight of the previous nine presidential elections and most of the intervening midterm elections as well. That didn't happen by accident—and it has nothing to do with the abundance of water for which Minnesota is rightly known. Culture, tradition, education, sound laws, and competent election administration have all played a part in making Minnesota the State That Votes.[1]

I've not only observed those influences on Minnesota voting. I've lived them. And I like to think I helped shape them.

When I was born in Minneapolis on September 28, 1935, Minnesota was still a youngster among the United States, a mere seventy-seven years past its May 11, 1858, birthdate. The state's founding generation was gone by then, but many of the children and grandchildren of those first immigrants were still alive and influential in civic life. So were the ideas that the state's early white residents brought with them for organizing and operating a representative democracy.[2]

The first of those European Americans were predominantly Yankees—that is, New Englanders and New Yorkers, largely descended from the English men and women who emigrated to the American colonies in the seventeenth century. They were drawn to Minnesota in the late 1840s and after for much the same reason that motivated their parents' and grandparents' generations when they relocated to places that became Ohio, Indiana, Illinois, Michigan, and

Wisconsin. They weren't escaping religious persecution or oppressive tyranny. They moved west to make money on the land that was being taken from Indigenous peoples.

The area that became Minnesota Territory in 1849 was a promising place in which to pursue financial gain—especially for New Englanders who knew how to turn running water into fortunes. The only major waterfall in the upper Mississippi River channel is situated in what is now downtown Minneapolis. It had been called St. Anthony Falls by an early European visitor, Father Louis Hennepin, in 1680, and the name stuck. The village that sprang up on the east bank of the falls also took the name St. Anthony. By the time statehood was granted, it was populated by people seeking to make money either by using rushing water to power lumber, flour, and textile mills, or by supplying inputs for those enterprises. That same year, 1858, the town of Minneapolis was organized on the west side of the falls. By 1872, St. Anthony had merged with Minneapolis, whose rapid growth and industrial prowess would soon surpass that of the older city downriver that had become the state's capital, St. Paul.[3]

The New Englanders brought with them a tradition of broad citizen participation in government (by free, white males, of course) that political scientist Daniel Elazar in the twentieth century would call "moralistic." By that, he meant that Minnesotans and their New England forebears considered government a legitimate and effective tool for producing a better society. From that notion sprang the ideas that elective office is a high calling and the making of government through politics is an important activity, worthy of everyone's time and energy. In a moralistic political culture like Minnesota's, "politics is ideally a matter of concern and duty for every citizen," Elazar said.[4]

Those ideas can be traced at least to the failed Puritan rebellion against England's monarchy in the seventeenth century. The Puritan critics of the Anglican Church's elitism brought with them to the New World a preference for egalitarianism, simple living, hard work, and shared sacrifice for the sake of the common good. The New England towns they founded were governed by town meetings in which every adult male could vote and participate. The governments they created tended to be loaded with official positions—the New Hampshire Legislature is still the nation's largest, with 424 members—so that power was widely shared.

But it can be claimed that the ideas about democracy and society that the Puritans embraced originated elsewhere. The ancient Greeks inspired abiding interest in democratic rule. Closer to the British Isles, two Scandinavian island nations, Iceland and the Faroe Islands (now part of Denmark), created parliaments in the tenth century that continue to operate today. And the anti-hierarchical ideals of the Puritans were not greatly different from those of the new Protestant strain of Christianity that swept Scandinavia in the sixteenth and seventeenth centuries—Lutheranism.

That similarity would prove important 250 years later and a hemisphere away in Minnesota. When Scandinavians began to arrive in Minnesota in large numbers after the American Civil War, they reinforced the New England notions about community and government that were already in play in the young state. That was also true, though to a lesser extent, of those arriving in Minnesota from Germany, who by 1910 were second only to natives of Sweden among Minnesota's foreign-born residents. Political scientists have noted that a region's dominant political culture is determined by its earliest settlers. In early Minnesota, the mix of Yankee and Nordic ideas about government generated a strong preference for participatory democracy.[5]

In a roundabout way, my family is part of that story. My father, Arthur Ferdinand Anderson, was the son of a couple from Östergötland, a province in southeastern Sweden. Axel Ferdinand Anderson and Anna Charlotte Peterson met there and became engaged to marry in 1897. They were people of modest means who dreamed of building a prosperous life in America. Axel emigrated first, heading to Red Oak, Iowa, where his brother was already working as a farmhand and where he was assured of work at a fair wage. Anna came to the United States a year later, in 1898, when a cousin living in Connecticut helped pay for her passage. They worked hard in 1898 and 1899 to put aside enough money to rent a farm and begin a household, and they were married in Wales, Iowa, on March 7, 1900. Dad, the second of four children who survived infancy, was born three years later. When he was seventeen, he and his family moved to Buffalo, Minnesota.

Axel and Anna Anderson, my father's parents, peeling potatoes at their home in Red Oak, Iowa, about 1918

My mother, Lucille Mary Brown, also came to Minnesota as a youngster. She was born near Turtle Lake, Wisconsin, to a family with German, Irish, and Scottish ancestry and some Yankee roots too. My maternal grandfather, Alexander "Sandy" Brown, was a railroad switchman; in 1905, he married my grandmother Augusta Cecilia Quade, a woman of German ancestry born in Mound, Minnesota. My mom, called Brownie by the time I knew her, was the third of their four children, and was two years old when her family moved to Minneapolis.[6]

Both sides of my family were populated by people of modest means who worked hard, doted on their families, and worshipped regularly in their churches. Dad's church was initially Swedish Mission Covenant, later Presbyterian; Mom's was Roman Catholic, the church in which I was raised. All of them cared deeply about their communities. They faithfully voted in every election, volunteered in the community, read the newspaper, and occasionally talked politics. But running for office or working on a political campaign was not part of their story—not yet, anyway.

My father, Art Anderson, and his younger brother Russ, painting the barn, about 1916

My grandmother Augusta Quade Brown holding me; her father, Stephen Quade; and my mother, Lucille Mary Brown, 1936

The dawn of the Great Depression inspired my relatives to work and pray all the harder. It may even have convinced a few Republicans on the Anderson side to break with their pattern and vote for a Democrat for president, Franklin Roosevelt, or a Farmer-Labor Party governor, Floyd B. Olson—though they never confessed as much to me. But the Depression didn't suppress romance. Arthur, a shoe salesman and a graduate of Minneapolis Business School, and Lucille, a registered nurse trained at Eitel Hospital and living with other nurses in an Eitel dormitory, met at a party in Minneapolis. They were married in November 1933. I was born nearly two years later—at Eitel Hospital, naturally. As was customary for women then in far too many occupations, my birth ended Mom's nursing career. Today, I live just a few blocks from the old Eitel Hospital building on Loring Park (and yes, there's some debate about how far I have come in life).

• • •

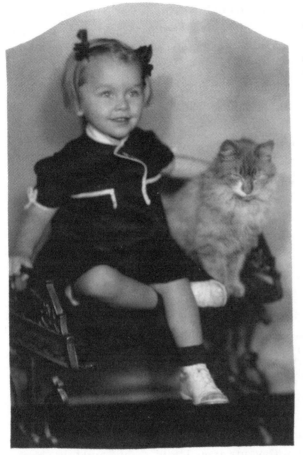

Posing at age two. Our neighbor ran a photography studio, and I was one of her models.

Mom and Dad took me home to a twin bungalow house at 4531 Fifteenth Avenue South, in blue-collar south-central Minneapolis. When I was two, we moved to a house at 3765 Kipling Avenue in St. Louis Park. That was my girlhood home. My brother and only sibling, Bill, joined us there in 1940. Dad had a number of jobs, but during World War II he was employed by Northern Pump Company, which had been created in 1929 from the merger of two Minneapolis businesses, Northern Fire Apparatus Company and Pagel Pump Company. In 1941, Dad's commute was lengthened when the company moved to Fridley; in 1942, his work changed again when Northern

Pump created a subsidiary named Northern Ordnance and began producing giant guns for US Navy warships. Dad's work included night shifts, which may have been a factor in his desire to make a change.[7]

Dad was drawn to Buffalo, the small town forty miles northwest of Minneapolis where his parents had moved in his late teens. It's now a Twin Cities bedroom community, with upward of twenty thousand residents. But in the 1940s it was a classic American small town, home to seventeen hundred people who knew each other well and patronized locally owned businesses on Main Street. The franchise for the Buffalo Gamble Store, part of the Minnesota-based Gamble Auto Supply retail chain, was for sale in 1945. My parents bought it.[8]

I was a fourth grader who loved my school, loved my friends, loved my knotty-pine bedroom under the eaves in our little St. Louis Park house, and hated to move. My mother, a lifelong city dweller, likely shared some of my sentiment. She had graduated from Minneapolis South High School, one of the largest in the state, and had been a speed skater before becoming a nurse. To her, Buffalo had to have been a backwater place, though it wasn't her nature to complain. She became acquainted in her new hometown through church and school activities, and she volunteered at my St. Francis Elementary School when the services of a nurse were required, as they were during the polio epidemics of the late 1940s. Once a year, she and Dad would drive to Minneapolis to shop at Dayton's annual "jubilee sale" and bring home a new dress for me. That was always a big treat for me and likely for her too, since she routinely sewed the rest of my wardrobe.

Dad flourished in Buffalo. He knew all of his customers in no time. He joined the brand-new Lions Club, ushered at the Presbyterian church, played cards with fellows he knew, and volunteered for community projects, all the while keeping shop six days a week and doing the store's bookkeeping on Sundays. He kept an old heating stove in the rear of the hardware store and hosted impromptu gatherings around it on cold days to discuss "the news"—much as a drugstore owner named Hubert H. Humphrey Sr. famously did not long before in Doland, South Dakota, while his namesake son and future US vice president listened and learned. I was aware of such

In my school uniform, about 1943

gatherings and might have eavesdropped a time or two, but I mostly kept my distance.

Among the men who sometimes joined that circle was the local state senator, Thomas Welch. He was a successful attorney who would serve twenty-four years in the Minnesota Senate and chair its judiciary committee, and he owned the fanciest house in town. In many places, that would have put him in a social stratum well removed from a shopkeeper like my father. But this was Minnesota, where Yankee and Scandinavian egalitarianism prevailed. Art Anderson and Tom Welch were friends, and Tom's daughter Susie was my schoolmate. Dad supported Tom's campaigns. Welch was part of the conservative caucus in the legislature, whose members were elected and served without party designation for sixty years, from 1913 to 1973. Caucusing with the conservatives meant that Welch was, in all likelihood, a Republican. So was my dad. In fact, so were all the businessfolk in Buffalo, as far as I could tell.

The Republican Party had been dominant in Minnesota politics since statehood. Minnesota became a state three years before the Civil War, and from the start, the state was caught up in the partisan battle over slavery and the Union's future. The state's first governor, Henry H. Sibley, was a Democrat. But two years later he was replaced by Republican Alexander Ramsey, who was the first governor in any state to offer troops to President Abraham Lincoln in April 1861 after Fort Sumter was shelled by Confederates and the war was on. Ramsey was the first of a long line of Republican governors; that party would hold state government's executive office for seventy-eight of the next one hundred years.

Republicans were the antislavery and pro-Union party, positions that gave them an electoral edge in Minnesota for the remainder of the nineteenth century. Scandinavian immigrants gravitated to the "Party of Lincoln" and found a welcome there. Minnesota elected Norwegian immigrant Knute Nelson governor in 1892, just thirty-four years after statehood, and proceeded to choose Scandinavian immigrants or their sons as governors and US senators for most of the next one hundred years. In the twentieth century, some splintering of Scandinavian-Minnesotans' partisan loyalties occurred, as economic forces battered both small farmers and working people and led to the creation of the Farmer-Labor (FL) Party, which had its heyday in the 1930s. The FL merged with the state's Democrats to create Minnesota's Democratic-Farmer-Labor (DFL) Party in 1944, and soon thereafter it began to give Republicans real competition. But small entrepreneurs like my dad stuck with the Grand Old Party (GOP), appreciative of its reputation for middle-class respectability and its view that the primary role of government was to help businesses thrive.

I was in high school when Dad ran for and won a seat on the Buffalo City Council, in 1951. Two years later, as I was preparing to graduate from high school, he ran for mayor and won. He would serve as Buffalo's mayor for ten years. Frankly, his campaigns had little effect on me. Life was casual in Buffalo then, and so were my dad's campaigns for office. I never saw a brochure or a lawn sign bearing his name. He would have considered such spending an extravagance. I don't think I ever door-knocked for him; I'm not sure he campaigned that way either. Dad's idea of campaigning was to do what he always did—walk around Buffalo and talk to people. By 1951, after sixteen years in business downtown, he had a lot of friends. People remembered when he extended them credit until a crop or a paycheck came in, or when he put off repossessing something they could not afford until after the holidays. He well understood the lean financial circumstances of many of his customers. He knew that they needed reliable basics, not frills, from city government.

Probably more than he knew, my calm and steady father taught me a lot about leadership in the public arena. He instilled in me a sense of responsibility for the community. He helped me see government as a natural extension of community life, not as an alien force to be feared or resented. He exhibited respect and consideration for the people he served, putting up with their dinner-hour calls about lost dogs or cats in trees without complaint. He showed me that running for office isn't the purview of an elite political class. Ordinary citizens of good will are needed in elective roles too, and can serve very well. Extraordinary personal abilities or resources aren't as important as a willingness to work hard, a knack for building and maintaining positive personal relationships, and a sincere desire to build a better community. A big ego and deep pockets aren't required. Dad had neither. Yet he was a successful mayor, credited years later for bringing industry to town and improving public safety with measures such as better downtown lighting.

I'm glad I had him as a role model for public service, because I certainly did not have a female one. As I grew up, I did not know of a single woman in any elective office, local, state, or federal. In 1935, the year I was born, there were two women serving in the legislature: House members Mabeth Hurd Paige and Hannah Jensen Kempfer. Both had been elected in 1922, the first year that women were eligible to run for state offices. They had left office by the time I was ten and we moved to Buffalo. No woman took their places at the state capitol for the next six years. Thirty years after the suffrage fight ended, feminist passions had cooled in Minnesota and much of the rest of the country. It wasn't clear when—or whether—they would return.[9]

Government and politics weren't the only careers that then appeared closed to women, of course. Our high school counselor told us girls we could be secretaries, teachers, or nurses—and that's all. In my graduating class of seventy-nine students, no girls opted to pursue anything else. I thought I had no other option. I had been a good student. Though I was a bit shy, I was involved, as most of us town kids were, in extracurricular activities like drama, band, and yearbook. (Most of the farm kids had to catch the bus and hurry home for chores.) But no one at school—where most of my teachers were men—encouraged me to think expansively about college or career possibilities.

I got more encouragement—if you can call it that—at home. Mom always said in a manner that brooked no discussion: "You are going to college." She would sometimes add an explanation for her insistence: "If something were to happen to your husband, you'll need something to fall back on." She was referring to the possibility of widowhood or a breadwinner's disability, not divorce. All of my friends but one lived with both of their biological parents, and their mothers did not work outside the home. In Brownie Anderson's mid-twentieth-century Minnesota, sending a daughter off to college was the equivalent of taking out an insurance policy. Prudence dictated that I should not face the vagaries of adulthood without it.

Thus, my path was clear. I would go to college to prepare to be a teacher. It looked better to me than being a nurse or secretary. The obvious postsecondary choice was the affordable one nearby with a good reputation for teacher education: St. Cloud State Teachers College.[10]

2

What's a Government For?

I was grateful that St. Cloud State Teachers College was available just thirty-five miles from home—grateful for its quality, its affordability, and the fact that it kept me near a boyfriend from Buffalo. I'm not sure that I was consciously grateful to state government for giving me that option.

Though I was a mayor's daughter, we didn't talk a great deal about government at home. We subscribed to the weekly *Buffalo Journal* but not to a daily newspaper, which my frugal parents would have considered an extravagance. My parents listened to Cedric Adams read the news on WCCO radio at ten each weeknight, but I was usually in bed by that hour—and likely would not have found them eager to discuss the news if I had been by their sides. I was aware that taxpayer support was a factor in keeping tuition rates low at St. Cloud and its four sister teachers' colleges in Winona, Moorhead, Mankato, and Bemidji. As a regular, churchgoing Catholic, I had at one point considered enrolling in the Jesuit-founded Marquette University in Milwaukee, Wisconsin, until I discovered how much more expensive that school would be.[1]

I would have been hard-pressed as a teenager to say much about the ways in which government as practiced in Minnesota had enriched my life. It was taken for granted that every little town like mine would be served by a paved highway; that law enforcers and firefighters would respond quickly to any emergency call; that drinking water would be clean and unfailingly available; that a family need not be impoverished by the need to care for a mentally ill or disabled relative.

And that at the heart of every town, almost as if placed there by a force of nature, there would be a public school.

My schoolmates and I could take public education for granted in the mid-twentieth century because the people who settled in Minnesota a hundred years earlier had not. Those New Englanders took their cue from the Northwest Ordinance of 1787, a remarkable piece of legislation enacted by Congress five months before the US Constitution was ratified. It bore a strong New England stamp. Its far-reaching provisions described how the territory north and west of the Ohio River—then occupied by many Indigenous nations, soon to be taken through treaties, and including a portion of what is now Minnesota—would be organized, governed, and eventually admitted to the Union as several states. Included in the guidance it gave those who planned to move there: "Religion, morality and knowledge being necessary to good government and the happiness of mankind, schools and the means of education shall forever be encouraged."[2]

Minnesota's territorial legislature took those words to heart. Among its first acts in 1849 was the decree that common schools were to be created and open without charge to all persons between ages four and twenty-one, to be supported by a statewide property tax and a slice of funds generated by criminal fines and liquor licenses. In 1858, the new state legislature appointed the first state superintendent of schools. In 1861, the legislature specified that every township in the state—eventually more than twenty-seven hundred—would be required to operate a school. That was soon deemed unworkable. In 1862, a more practical system of school districts and elected school boards was established that continues to this day.[3]

It must be acknowledged that despite their lofty intentions, Minnesotans did not always live up to their public-education promises. Schools were established throughout the state according to plan. But in the first seventy-five years of statehood, very little state money followed, even though the state constitution made the legislature—not local governments—responsible for a "general and uniform system of public schools," to be supported by "taxation or otherwise as will secure a thorough and efficient system of public schools throughout the state." During the Great Depression, many schools in rural areas found themselves unable to pay their teachers because farmers were unable to pay their local property taxes. That predicament led to the creation of Minnesota's first state income tax in 1933, dedicated by statute to public education. It can be argued that that move was the crucial first step in the creation of modern Minnesota. By the time I was a student at Buffalo High School, Minnesota was on its way to tying school funding—and thus school quality—to the state's economy and its collective political judgment, not local wealth or whim.[4]

That shift in state education funding policy made the 1950s a propitious time to begin a career in teaching. So did the arrival of the generation that followed mine. The baby boom that began after World War II was in full swing in the 1950s, packing elementary schools to capacity and stretching thin the state's teaching resources. I enrolled in an elementary teacher education sequence that allowed me to take classes in the summer and graduate in three years. It put me into a classroom even sooner, via a student teaching program that was considered state of the art. By the time I was twenty, I was living on my own and student teaching in Princeton. That may seem abrupt by today's standards. But before the 1950s, teachers employed in much of rural America had far less preparation than I had—often as little as a single year of post–high school education at a so-called normal school.

I enjoyed student teaching. But I wasn't anticipating a long career in education. I was confident that my future entailed marriage and motherhood, with my education degree available to dust off only in case of emergency. I could not—or did not want to—imagine any alternative future.

I met my first husband when he was a student at St. Thomas College (today's University of St. Thomas) in St. Paul, and he was in St. Cloud for a sporting event. Ours was mostly a correspondence courtship, with intermittent visits. I would go to Minneapolis to spend the weekend with my grandparents on Thirteenth Avenue South, reserving Saturday nights for him. He would find an excuse to come to St. Cloud on Friday or Saturday and stay until Sunday. It wasn't quite a whirlwind romance. But we did not know each other nearly well enough when we married on August 18, 1956, just three months after I graduated. We were both just twenty years old. My husband had another year ahead of him at St. Thomas and planned to go to law school after that. I would start married life as our household's breadwinner. A few days after our wedding, I reported for duty as an elementary school teacher in Bloomington, a sprawling, rapidly growing suburb south of Minneapolis.

The first of the baby boomers were ten years old in 1956. Elementary schools—especially suburban ones like mine—were overwhelmed. To cope, Bloomington Public Schools ran two class sessions per day, morning and afternoon. I taught second graders in the afternoon session, which meant my students were at their desks from noon until 4 PM. These were youngsters who only a few years before had been taking naps at that time of day. I remember how tired many of them looked by 4 PM! I wasn't too happy at that hour either, knowing that I had a rush-hour drive ahead of me from Bloomington to our rented, upstairs duplex in south Minneapolis.

I didn't have to put up with that commute for long. We found an inexpensive converted chicken coop to rent behind a house in Bloomington. The following year, my husband enrolled at the University of Minnesota Law School. But I wasn't back to work in the classroom. I was pregnant, and that meant the end of my employment as a teacher. I found a job as a part-time grocery store cashier until baby Michael came in December 1958. My husband's law-student status and Michael's birth made us eligible for married-student housing—essentially barracks, divided into small apartments with a living room, two bedrooms, and a tiny kitchen—near the University of Minnesota's St. Paul campus. That was still our home when our daughter Colleen came in 1959.

By the time David, our third child, was born thirteen months after Colleen, my husband had completed law school. We moved to an apartment in Northeast Minneapolis while he looked for work. Finding few opportunities in the Twin Cities, he cast his eyes 160 miles west to his hometown, Tracy, Minnesota. He could set up a solo practice, he explained, and provide our children with an idyllic-sounding small-town childhood among his family and friends.

In 1960, Tracy had nearly six hundred more people than the small town I knew best, Buffalo. But it was far removed from anything familiar to me. My husband's father was deceased; my mother-in-law ran a modest boardinghouse, where we found temporary lodging as we relocated. My husband's unmarried aunt, who worked at a jewelry store, provided us with some financial support. I understood how my own mother must have felt fifteen years earlier when she was uprooted from the Twin Cities to Buffalo. Following her example—and encumbered by the daily demands of motherhood—I resolved to make the best of my new situation.

My husband made that increasingly difficult. I knew he drank to excess on occasion in college and law school, but I assumed that was because of the stress of his studies. Unfortunately, his drinking intensified when he was back in Tracy. People there thought it was wonderful that a native son had gone to law school in the Twin Cities and come home to make a career. They wanted him to succeed. They would tend to look the other way—and not tell me (at least, not right away)—when they would find him drunk on the streets late at night. Sometimes, his softball buddies would bring him home, aiming to protect me. Other times, it was the police who got him home—or the police who would keep him in their custody until he sobered up. I did my part in the community's conspiracy of silence. I said nothing about his constant physical abuse after his drinking episodes. But I began to worry about my three children. I wondered what would happen to them if I didn't wake up some morning.

I also became increasingly aware that my husband's drinking was consuming a large share of the little money he was making as a lawyer. We were charging everything we bought. When winter was upon us and we needed fuel oil in the tank that fed our furnace, the man who came to pump in a few gallons said to me, "You know, your husband owes me a lot of money. But I don't want your children to be cold." I heard a similar line at the grocery store as I signed for purchases, which small-town grocers allowed in those days. One day the grocer said as he extended me credit, "We want you to be able to feed your children." I was mortified—and, for a time, paralyzed. Excessive drinking was considered a moral flaw, a shameful thing not to be discussed. I didn't even know the word *alcoholism* in those years.

Neither had I heard anyone speak openly about domestic abuse. I surely didn't know how prevalent such abuse was, or how to seek help. Shelters for abuse victims and their children were not yet in existence. A priest in another town with whom I sought counsel told me my husband's drinking was my cross to bear. With no money and three children under age four, I thought I had little choice but to try to bear it. When someone would ask me about a bruise on my face, I'd give a nervous laugh and say, "Oh, I bumped into something." People in town must have thought I was exceedingly clumsy.

After months of suffering in silence, I had to tell my parents. They visited us frequently and, noticing our empty cupboards, brought us food. They arrived with toys for the children at Christmas—but my husband didn't. When he failed to come home on Christmas Eve or Christmas Day, I could not make excuses for him any longer. I told my mom and dad everything, including the fact that I had been secretly squirrelling away small amounts of household money to finance an escape. I had amassed a small fortune—$78.

My parents came back the next day to take me and the children home to Buffalo. A short time later, we returned to Tracy. My husband made promises, and I wanted to try once more to be a functional family. But it was in vain. When I left the next time a few months later, I knew it was for good. I left my children with sympathetic in-laws and said I would be back as soon as I found a job and a place for us to live. Leaving that marriage was one of the hardest things I've ever done. But I truly believed I was saving my children's lives, and my own. And I have never looked back on that decision.

● ● ●

I took the bus to Minneapolis and started looking for a teaching job that would sustain me and three small children. But I had not acquired the continuing education credits then required to maintain one's teaching license. Mine had lapsed. I turned to my Catholic roots and found a job in St. Paul at Christ Child School for Exceptional Children. I did so with some trepidation, since I had no experience working with children with developmental disabilities. But the nun in a wheelchair who ran the school was a feisty, bighearted woman who inspired confidence. "I'll teach you all you need to know," she assured me. The $300-per-month salary that job paid was a lifeline. I found a duplex to rent across the street from a grocery store and on the school bus route that served the school—important considerations, since I had no car and relied on that bus to get to work each morning. With those arrangements made, I eagerly fetched my kids from Tracy and started life as a single parent.

Soon thereafter, I filed for divorce. When my case came before Judge Walter Mann in Lyon County District Court, Dad drove me to Marshall, the Lyon County seat, for the hearing. We were obliged to take my eldest, Michael, with us—Mom was willing to watch two but not three active young children. Walter Mann was a legendary judge in that part of the state; his wife, Polly, would eventually become even better known as an antiwar activist. Judge Mann was extraordinarily kind to me that day. My guess is that he was already aware of my husband's chemical dependency and violent behavior. By then, it seemed that everyone in Lyon County knew. Judge Mann said, "Let's close the courtroom." He did not want me to have to air our family's dirty laundry in public. He took a look at Michael and said, "Somebody get a cot for this little boy. He needs a nap." I had a lawyer to make my case; my ex-husband represented himself. The case was straightforward and quickly decided. I was awarded alimony, child support, and total custody of the children. Of course, I never saw a penny of the money I had been awarded. I never expected to. I only wanted my husband out of our lives—and my only regret was not leaving him sooner.[5]

I was relieved to be out of danger and proud of the independence I'd exhibited—more than ever previously in my life. But I was also embarrassed and exhausted. My fate was unlike anyone else's I then knew. I did not have sympathetic friends in whom I could confide. I had no regret about leaving Tracy. But the unfairness of my circumstances grated on me. I had not caused my predicament. I had done nothing wrong. I was the victim, yet my children and I were punishingly poor.

We were lucky to live across the street from a grocery store. I would buy three pork chops, one for each of my children, and make a meal for myself with whatever they left on their plates. I lusted after

Before dinner at my parents' house, about 1965, when Michael was six, Colleen five, and David four. My brother took the photo.

the women's magazines in that grocery store, but never bought one. They cost a precious twenty-five cents.

My mom bought me a brown, shirtwaist dress that I wore every day to work. It was the only dress I had. The day its belt broke was a sad day indeed! I found a babysitter nearby who had a child of her own and would watch my children after school and in the evening so that I could enroll at the University of Minnesota's College of Education. That would get me the credits I needed to be certified to teach in public school. My rent was $125 per month; the babysitter cost $100 per month. That left me $75 to cover everything else, every month, through the nine-month school year. It was tough. My parents, bless them, brought food when they came to visit. And Mom worked wonders on her sewing machine, just as she had done for me when I was a girl. I don't think I bought a single garment for my kids for ten years.

Things got worse before they got better. I was required to take additional courses to reinstate my teaching certificate. I enrolled at the University of Minnesota and took evening courses throughout the 1963–64 school year. That allowed me to land a job for the next school year teaching mentally challenged children at St. Anthony Public Schools, adjacent to Northeast Minneapolis. I found a duplex to rent near Central Avenue in Columbia Heights. But I had no income in the summer of 1964. I had no choice but to apply for welfare, then called Aid to Families with Dependent Children, or AFDC.

It was a humiliating experience that I tried hard to avoid. But I couldn't find a summer job that would pay enough to allow me to hire a babysitter. A neighbor told me that I should go to the Hennepin County Courthouse to apply for help. I was mortified at the thought, but when it became clear that the alternative was hunger and homelessness, I did it. I saw it as a necessary bridge that would allow me and the children to safely get from one job to another.

Not long after I applied, a young social worker came to my house to assess my circumstances and give me suggestions about how to save money. It was insulting to hear a bunch of worthless tips from someone younger than me who had no idea what I'd been through. Soon thereafter, I received coupons from the county that could be redeemed for bulk quantities of such staples as flour and cornmeal. The coupons could be used at only a few locations. I remember trekking to a store on Central Avenue with three small children in tow to pick up foodstuffs for which I had little practical use, in quantities that were difficult to get home. Never again would I tolerate any suggestion that people "on the dole" have it easy!

When the new school year started and my paychecks resumed, I got off AFDC as quickly as possible. That's what most Minnesotans on welfare do, I learned later. A 2006 study found that seven out of ten families on today's version of AFDC, the Minnesota Family Investment Program, after three years had either left the program or were working at least thirty hours a week and were nearing an exit.[6]

The following year, my life gained some stability. I enjoyed my year of teaching at St. Anthony Public Schools. I found a wonderful woman on my block who would care for my children while I was at work. And I finally had a little time for a social life of my own. A friend introduced me to Glen Growe, a marketing specialist, who was fun to be with and liked being with my kids.

In June 1965, I married Glen, and we moved to Burnsville, where I did some substitute teaching. I had a house in the suburbs and a husband who went to work every day and who treated me well. I had finally achieved the conventional life I had once planned. At last, I felt like a normal person.

Though my years in poverty and my stay on AFDC were short, those experiences had an enduring effect on me. Those lean years made me tougher, more independent and resilient. I became more pragmatic and less sentimental. And my understanding of the role of government changed. Before, government to me was my dad, running a little town in a very congenial way, looking out for things like stop signs, lost pets, and snowplowing. My summer on AFDC showed me that government could do more and should do more. When trouble comes in people's lives, families aren't always there or aren't always able to help; communities aren't always reliably compassionate or capable. Government is the only force big enough and dependable enough to provide a sure rescue when life's vagaries land people in impossibly tough spots. Government had been a stabilizer for me when I really needed one. I became convinced it ought to be there for others too.

Now I saw that government provided much on which I had previously relied without giving it a thought. When my paychecks resumed, I looked at the line for state tax deductions with fresh appreciation. When I discovered the next year that I would receive a state income tax refund, I was amazed, and half tempted to turn it down! I didn't—I needed the money. But I also knew well that state government was using my tax dollars to help others just like me who were in need. State government was an enterprise that had earned my gratitude and deserved my support.

3

Riding the Second Wave

In 1966, I was no bored housewife like those described in Betty Friedan's 1963 book *The Feminine Mystique.* I was a newly remarried
wife, busy mom, occasional substitute teacher, and new resident of
suburban Burnsville. But I was looking for opportunities to become
involved in my community. I opted to join the League of Women
Voters.[1]

I'm not sure whether the notion of joining the league originated
with me or someone else's suggestion. If it was the latter, I owe that
person a debt of gratitude. Joining the League of Women Voters was
one of the best decisions I ever made. The league changed my life.

The change-making potency of the League of Women Voters comes
as no surprise to anyone familiar with its history. It's the organization
that sprang directly from the solidarity, grit, and organizational skills
of the feminist crusaders who won the right to vote for American
women in 1920, after a tenacious, seventy-year struggle. (At least, for
white American women; African American women would have the
nominal right to vote, but in some parts of the country they would
not be able to exercise that right until the 1960s.) The national league
was born eighteen months before the ratification of the Nineteenth
Amendment to the US Constitution, at a convention of the National
American Woman Suffrage Association. Victory was not yet in hand
when that decision was made. But the goal was tantalizingly close.
That year, the suffrage association's leader, Carrie Chapman Catt,
had engineered a merger with an eight-year-old competing organization, the National Council on Women Voters. That group's focus was
the motivation and education of newly enfranchised female voters

in those states (Minnesota was not among them) that had already granted women the right to vote. The merger signified that the suffrage association had no intention to disband after winning the vote. It would continue what Catt called a "mighty political experiment" to help women exercise their electoral power. A new name—the League of Women Voters—was intended to convey that message. The 1919 convention of the suffrage association initiated the merger; the 1920 convention put the league's bylaws and officers in place.[2]

By then, Minnesota had finally joined the women's suffrage bandwagon. For all its Yankee and Scandinavian devotion to participatory democracy, Minnesota had been in no hurry to extend the right to vote to women. Like several other states—and at the urging of Mahala Fisk Pillsbury, the state's first lady at the time—Minnesota allowed women to vote in school board elections beginning in 1875. But that's as much loosening of the male grip on power that Minnesotans would permit until March 1919, the very month in which the first steps were taken to create the national League of Women Voters. On March 24, the legislature granted women the right to vote for presidential electors, beginning in the 1920 presidential election. On September 8 that year, the legislature met in special session to ratify the Nineteenth Amendment, which had been sent to the states that June. And on October 29, 1919, the Minnesota Woman Suffrage Association formally dissolved and reconstituted itself as a state branch of the national League of Women Voters.[3]

Catt's prediction that the league would be the vanguard of a "mighty political experiment" after women won the vote proved too optimistic. To be sure, Minnesota saw a burst of female political activity immediately after the battle was won. One Minnesota town, blue-collar meat-packing headquarters South St. Paul, welcomed women to the polls on August 27, 1920, just one day after US Secretary of State Bainbridge Colby signed a proclamation granting American women the constitutional right to vote. The city scheduled a waterworks bond-issue election for that day in the hope of being recognized as the first in the state to allow women to vote in municipal elections. The gimmick worked unexpectedly well. National news organizations sent reporters to witness eighty-seven women legally casting votes for the first time. A story ran in the nationally circulating *Saturday Evening Post* magazine, and Fox movie theaters around the country showed newsreels for weeks thereafter of South St. Paul women in line at the polls.[4]

In 1922, the first year in which women could run for statewide office, eight women sought seats in the Minnesota House, and four of them won—Hannah Jensen Kempfer of Ottertail County; and Mabeth Hurd Paige, Sue Metzger Dickey Hough, and Myrtle Cain of Minneapolis.

Unfortunately, the initial surge of feminist political enthusiasm didn't last. Cain and Hough would be gone after the 1924 election. When Kempfer and Paige finally retired, the Minnesota Legislature was without any female representatives for three terms, from 1945 to 1951. Only a few women held legislative seats in the next twenty years. Minnesota had no female district court judges and very few elected city and county officials in those years. The state's first female member of Congress, Democrat Coya Knutson, was defeated after two terms when political enemies in her own party convinced her estranged alcoholic husband, Andy, to publicly plead, "Coya, come home!" If feminist sentiment in Minnesota were measured by a line graph through the years, that year—1958—might have been its nadir.

It says something about the staying power of the League of Women Voters that it survived the economic privations of the 1930s, the upheavals of the 1940s, and the domesticity that literally birthed the baby boom in the 1950s. But the league did not thrive everywhere in the state. By the 1950s, its chapters were concentrated in Minneapolis and a few college towns in Greater Minnesota. It's likely no coincidence that where the league was active, women could still win an occasional legislative seat in the 1950s and 1960s. For example, state representatives Sally Luther, elected in 1950, and Alpha Smaby, elected in 1965, sprang from parts of Minneapolis where league chapters were vigorous. Representative Helen McMillan of Austin—the only woman in the legislature in the late 1960s—was a past president of the state League of Women Voters.

As the Twin Cities suburbs swelled in the 1960s, new league chapters were born and dormant ones revived. The chapter in Burnsville was eager to grow, which meant its members were especially welcoming. I considered the league the most important group a woman could join. The Burnsville chapter was largely comprised of well-educated women who did not work outside their homes but who wanted to make an impact on their community. They met and worked on league projects during daytime hours while their children were in school. The work included intellectually challenging studies of government policies—state and local matters like housing, metropolitan governance, and access to the ballot. Those study groups led to policy recommendations and opportunities to lobby at the state capitol and city halls. The work was strictly nonpartisan. Both Republicans and DFLers were league members, and the league very consciously avoided taking sides with one party over another.

Joining the Burnsville league chapter was like handing me a little piece of heaven. I was welcomed with open arms and given a chance to meet people from throughout the community. The work was confidence-building. It schooled me on the civic issues of the day and gave me a chance to discuss them with people in positions of power. Before I knew it, I was in charge of organizing debates among local political candidates. I became acquainted with a lot of local leaders and up-and-comers, both candidates and their aides.

I also agreed to help with a voter registration project that involved going to Parent-Teacher Association (PTA) meetings and inviting people to register. In the 1960s, Minnesota did not yet allow voters to register on Election Day, so prior registration was essential to exercising one's franchise. Making registration readily available was particularly important in a suburb with a growing population of newcomers— something I understood personally! Yet offering people a chance to register at a site other than a city hall or county courthouse was a novelty. We leaguers had to be registered as deputy city clerks and to get the PTA's permission to set up a table at its meetings—and in so doing, we attracted the attention of the local newspaper. We welcomed the publicity. "It's all to promote citizen participation," we said whenever we were asked. I was becoming passionate about that cause.

• • •

Another cause was capturing my attention at the same time. In 1967—as I was caring for our infant son, Patrick, born that March—I found myself increasingly alarmed by American involvement in the Vietnam War. I was appalled by the images I was seeing each night on television news of young American soldiers, most of them draftees, both in harm's way and inflicting harm on innocent people in a place that seemed far removed from our national interest. American involvement in that war struck me as Yankee paternalism. The United States didn't have any business injecting itself into that nation's civil war, I thought—and history should have taught us that these ventures usually don't end well. With Patrick's arrival, I was the mother of three sons. I saw the Vietnam War with a mother's eyes. Before long, I had put a badge reading "Another mother for peace" around my neck and had signed on to support the antiwar presidential candidacy of Minnesota senator Eugene McCarthy.

Though McCarthy had been a Minnesota senator since 1958 and a congressman for a decade before that, he wasn't especially well known to me before 1967. Like many DFL politicians in the 1950s and 1960s, he had spent his political life in the shadow of Hubert H. Humphrey, the engineer of the 1944 Democratic and Farmer-Labor parties' merger and the state's best-known politician. But when, as vice president, Humphrey stayed loyal to President Lyndon Johnson's war policy in 1966 and 1967, McCarthy asserted his independence. He was one of the US Senate's most outspoken critics of the war before finally announcing on November 15, 1967, that he would challenge Johnson for the presidency with the aim of ending US involvement in Vietnam.

By that time, war opponents were recruiting like-minded participants for the state's partisan precinct caucuses, set for March 5, 1968. The goal was to elect delegates to future party conventions who supported McCarthy's candidacy. I met him personally for the first time at a pre-caucus coffee party in Edina, and was impressed with his principled views and scholarly demeanor. The fact that, like me, he was a Catholic from Greater Minnesota gave me more reason to like him.

I did not need much convincing to attend my first-ever DFL pre-cinct caucus. It did not matter to me that I had been raised in a Re-publican household or that I had no prior connection to the DFL Party. Neither did it matter that as an officer in the League of Women Voters, I could not assume a DFL Party office or become a delegate myself. I saw myself as a league person, not a DFLer. My only inten-tion in attending caucuses that year was to hasten the end of Ameri-can involvement in Vietnam.

State DFL chairman Warren Spannaus, a Humphrey ally, predicted before the caucuses that McCarthy's forces would fare poorly in the party that Hubert had built. He was wrong. DFL rules then called for winner-take-all—that is, a majority could elect all the delegates allot-ted to each precinct. In my caucus and in dozens more like it through-out the metro area, McCarthy backers took charge. We controlled the delegate elections in Minneapolis, St. Paul, and the southern and west-ern metro suburbs, as well as a number of outstate cities. The headline in the next day's *Minneapolis Star* told the tale: "McCarthy Deals LBJ Camp Stiff Setback."[5]

The precinct caucus results provided a brief interlude of euphoria in what was otherwise a tragic year for both America and Minne-sota DFLers. Two assassinations—killing Dr. Martin Luther King Jr. on April 4 and Robert F. Kennedy on June 6—rocked the country. Lyndon Johnson surprised the nation on March 31 by declining to run for a second term, opening the door to Humphrey's presidential candidacy. McCarthy's campaign was overtaken first by Kennedy's, then by Humphrey's, sorely dividing the Minnesota DFL. McCar-thy's unwillingness to endorse Humphrey until the closing days of the 1968 campaign likely contributed to his defeat by Republican Rich-ard Nixon—a candidate who claimed he had a secret plan to end the Vietnam War but who pressed on with hostilities through most of his presidency. American troops didn't leave Vietnam until they were forced out in defeat in 1975, after Nixon had left office and more than fifty-eight thousand Americans had died.[6]

The sad year 1968 had an unexpected coda for our family: my hus-band Glen's employer informed us that his job required a transfer to Buffalo, New York. The following summer, we moved four kids plus a dog, a cat, and two rabbits in time for the older children to start school in Buffalo. My dad tried to cheer me by cracking wise about my affinity for Buffaloes. But I remembered my dismay at moving from St. Louis Park to Buffalo, Minnesota, in 1945, when I was about the same age as my three elder children were in 1969. One thing helped me stay positive: as soon as I could, I sought out and joined Buffalo's League of Women Voters chapter.

The whole family was relieved when Glen's work allowed us to return to Minnesota a little more than a year later. This time, we settled in Minnetonka, a mostly affluent west-metro suburb just east of the big lake with the same name. I quickly became the treasurer of Minnetonka's League of Women Voters unit—at a propitious time.

• • •

What historians now call the second wave of the American women's movement started in the late 1960s on the nation's culturally cutting-edge coasts. Borrowing grassroots organizing and protest tactics from the civil rights and antiwar movements, the new "women's libbers" were fifty years removed from the first wave of suffragists. The new movement set its sights on achieving more opportunity for women in the workplace—including government.

By the early 1970s, the second wave had reached Minnesota. Both in formal women's organizations like the League of Women Voters and in informal "consciousness-raising" sessions springing up around the state, women were coming together to decry a lack of opportunity in the workplace and to plot strategies for change. That was true as well in both political parties. But feminist zeal for reform may have been stronger within the DFL, where remarkable leaders like Arvonne Skelton Fraser and Koryne Horbal were agitating for change. A group of DFL women commissioned a report by University of Minnesota social work professor Esther Wattenberg on the role of women in 1970s legislative campaigns. The result was a report entitled "Women in the DFL: Present but Powerless?" that detailed the subservient roles women played and the false male belief that women liked things that way. That report was circulated at dozens of meetings around the state as women pondered how to claim more power.[7]

Only one woman—former state League of Women Voters president Helen McMillan—had been elected to the 201-member Minnesota Legislature in 1970. Only five women had run at all. A resolve to increase those numbers in 1972 took hold. I shared that determination. But in 1971 and early 1972, I had no idea that getting more women to run for office would mean getting *me* to run.

In addition to my league activities, I had plunged into the Parent-Teacher Association at my children's Groveland Elementary School, becoming first a room mother, then PTA copresident with my husband. That got me involved in the 1971 school board election in the Minnetonka school district. A number of other league members were, like me, former teachers. We had a clear favorite in the school board contest. Several of us went to work as volunteers on his campaign. Our candidate didn't win, but we gained important campaign experience. My friend Gretchen Fogo would come to call our campaign approach the Hopkins method—referring to intense door-to-door canvassing by well-organized volunteers in the portion of the school district situated within the Hopkins city limits. That kind of campaigning appealed to me. It generated high voter turnout, giving elections legitimacy as reflections of the people's will. It also made smart strategic use of a key resource most suburban women then had—free time while our children were in school.

My league work also taught me about another crucial component of political campaigns: fundraising. With some trepidation, we decided to ask prominent people in Minnetonka for donations to allow our chapter to step up its activities. On my list for a solicitation call was former Minnetonka mayor Bill Cooley, a prominent real estate developer and businessman. He was someone whose social circle was nowhere close to mine. But bolstered by the company of my politically active friend Janet Yonehiro (now Johns), a former president of our league chapter elected to the Minnetonka City Council in 1971, I made an appointment with Cooley. As professionally as we could, Janet and I made our case. We were thrilled to death when he gave us a sizeable donation. I learned that asking people for money for a good cause wasn't as scary as I had imagined. It was actually fun!

Those were great growth years for me. For the first time as an adult, I had the time and financial stability to work on causes of my own choosing. I learned to meet people, recruit volunteers, make a sales pitch, give a speech to a crowd, and confront or challenge people when necessary. I found the courage and resources to act on my values. For example, I enrolled four-year-old Patrick in a north Minneapolis preschool. I wanted him to learn at an early age that human beings come in a variety of colors, all of which deserve his respect. I thought that lesson might be harder to learn in all-white Minnetonka in the 1970s.

All of that happened while women like me were deemed "just housewives" by much of society. Admittedly, our race and economic status gave us privileges that we did not yet fully see. In those years— and unlike today—our families could thrive on the income of one breadwinner. From where we stood, we could only focus on the barriers that had been erected to keep us in our places. My friends and I began to imagine what it would take to change narrow-minded attitudes about women's worth. Almost unwittingly, we were becoming feminists.

● ● ●

The courts had given Minnesota a new legislative district map for the 1972 election, the first after the 1970 census had found substantial population growth in the Twin Cities' western suburbs. Redistricting created a new seat in Minnetonka and Eden Prairie, District 40A. Though the state legislature was still officially (and for the last time) nonpartisan in 1972, political party endorsement mattered— especially in a Republican-dominated district like mine. We "league ladies" knew that if we were to elect a woman to fill that open seat, we would be well advised to launch her candidacy by securing the Republican Party's endorsement. We had a very able candidate in Gwen Luhta, our league chapter president and the wife of an insurance executive. She was smart, well versed on the issues, an able speaker, and a proven leader. We deemed her much better qualified than her opponent, auto repair business owner Richard Stranik. Gwen resigned as our chapter's president to signal her commitment to running and serving in the state House. League members who were Republicans backed her. But she couldn't overcome Stranik's advantage as a party insider. He was that year's GOP's Third Congressional District chairman and a delegate to the 1972 Republican National Convention. Much to our chagrin, the endorsement went to him.

One of our League of Women Voters friends was Nancy Wangen, who was also the DFL Party's associate chair in our district. DFLers had not yet found a candidate in District 40A, she told the discouraged Luhta campaign team as they huddled after the GOP convention. The DFL endorsing convention was just days later. Gwen's bid for Republican endorsement made her a poor candidate for the DFL nod, Nancy said. But it would not do for Stranik to run unopposed. If he had an opponent from the league, he would be forced to study the issues to avoid embarrassing himself at the league-sponsored debate, she argued. Maybe he would learn something.

"How about Joan Growe?" someone suggested. When the meeting broke up, I had several calls from desperate leaguers asking me— please!—to consider running.

The thought had not occurred to me before. Now it did. I had become immersed in public policy at the league, and I enjoyed it. I'd been at the capitol for the league a few times and watched legislators in action. "I could do better than that," I thought when I heard ill-informed comments from legislators about policy matters the league had studied. I liked the idea of taking what was billed (somewhat inaccurately) as a part-time job, one that allowed for summers off with my family and considerable free time in odd-numbered autumns.

But I knew that District 40A leaned Republican. Even in an officially nonpartisan election, someone endorsed by the DFL would have an uphill battle. "Glen is out of town, and I don't have a speech prepared," I demurred—but I didn't say no. I told Nancy I'd think about it and give her an answer the next day—the day of the DFL convention.

That morning, Nancy called me for my answer. I told her if someone could find a babysitter for my children and write a speech for me, I would do it. Connie Hudnut found the babysitter. Nancy brought me the speech that Gwen had given two days before. It was written on recipe cards, with the word Republican crossed out and DFL scrawled instead. Using Gwen's speech to make my case, I was endorsed without opposition. It was over in a matter of minutes. Afterward, when I called Glen with the news, he mildly said, "Okay, that's fine." Neither of us knew what I had gotten into.

"Now what do I do?" I asked. The men who had been in charge of DFL matters in Minnetonka for years—and had yet to win a legislative election—puffed up with offers of advice. I invited them to my living room a few days later for a meeting. The longer they talked about money, issue papers, and endorsements, the more ill at ease I felt. They were telling me all that I had to do, but they were not offering to help. At the end of that meeting, the men simply wished me luck and left. Nancy Wangen stayed behind and handed me a check for something like $25 or $50. No one else did.

Gretchen Fogo was out of town that night. When she returned, I called her with an urgent plea: "Help! I am in such trouble!" Gretchen was more than a League of Women Voters friend. Like me, Gretchen is a former teacher; among the subjects she had taught were junior high school American history and civics. Like me, she had supported Eugene McCarthy's presidential candidacy in 1968. She truly believed my candidacy had value. She is also the most organized person I know. My queasy stomach started to settle when she agreed to join Nancy as cochair of my campaign.

With no one telling us how to proceed, Gretchen tackled our campaign as if she were designing the syllabus for a course, with lesson plans for each day and week. She invoked the Hopkins method we'd used on the school board race the previous year, with heavy reliance on door-to-door canvassing. We didn't have much money, but we had people power—or, more specifically, women power. Nancy and Gretchen recruited a core group of about a dozen volunteers, all stay-at-home mothers in their late thirties and forties, many allied with the League of Women Voters. Arranging babysitting was an essential component of our plan—which may have been a first for a Minnesota legislative campaign. The campaign team often met at St. Luke Presbyterian Church; the members hired a babysitter to watch their children as they met. They set goals and deadlines—so many houses visited by such-and-such date—and worked backward on the calendar. They soon had a daily campaign schedule that they considered daunting but doable. It gave me my daily marching orders.

The literature for my campaign did not mention that I had DFL endorsement. In fact, we made a point of listing the names of supporters who were Republicans and independents. When the state party asked, we agreed to distribute DFL Party literature at the doors, but decided to do so separately from our own. The same went for literature touting the presidential candidacy of George McGovern of South Dakota, who was headed for the only rejection Minnesota voters would give a Democratic candidate for president in more than a half century. We concluded that de-emphasizing my DFL connection was necessary for me to have a chance. In October, I told the *Minneapolis Star* that I would join the liberal caucus in the state House because "in our system you must get organized." But "after that, I don't have party ties or obligations and I'll vote the way I feel."[8]

We also didn't trumpet the fact that our campaign was a female-run affair. We decided to recruit a man, F. William Graham, to be our treasurer, putting his name in the fine print on our literature to soothe any donors who might think a man was needed to handle money. But we set the budget and raised money the way women's organizations did then, with bake sales, rummage sales, and pass-the-hat coffee parties. With little support from the skeptical men in the DFL, we lacked other options.

Other candidates in different districts dropped literature only at the doors of known supporters. That wasn't our plan. We set out to visit every house in the district, multiple times. Our team was large enough to assign one volunteer to every forty homes in the district. We asked each volunteer to call on her assigned households several times during the run of the campaign, plus host a meet-the-candidate coffee party, install lawn signs, and raise money. We did much of that work during daytime hours—times when few adults are at home today but a great time in 1972 for woman-to-woman campaigning. My job was to visit every household at least once. I was on the street every day, rain or shine, Monday through Saturday, from 9 AM to dark, and on Sundays, from noon until I could no longer see the house num-

Our campaign raised funds at events like this coffee party in a suburban home, 1972.

bers. My mom insisted that I buy and wear comfortable shoes. I wore a button that read, "A Woman's Place Is in the House."

It wasn't unusual for the people I met at the doors to assume that I was campaigning for my husband. They had never seen a woman candidate for the legislature before. It was also common for people to ask who would take care of my children if I won. I had a rehearsed response ready: "My youngest is about to start school and, like a lot of other women, I'm ready to go back to work. I want to work for you in state government." I'd generally add that serving in the legislature is a part-time job.

In my "free" time early in the morning or late in the evening, the campaign arranged for me to be briefed by experts on key issues. Our team wanted to be able to refute the claim that a woman candidate could not master legislative complexity. We honed in on the most complex state issue of the day—school finance. Governor Wendell

Anderson and the 1971 legislature had just enacted an overhaul of school finances that in later years would come to be called the Minnesota Miracle. It was not yet well understood by sitting legislators, let alone first-time candidates. The plan called for a big increase in state funding for school districts, with funds allocated according to a complicated scheme based on a district's student population and property tax capacity. The idea was to reduce property tax burdens, but to do so in a way that also closed the per-student funding gap between wealthy and poorer districts. Education was a big issue in my district. I supported that change, and I worked hard to become conversant with its aspects. With the help of my "tutor" Diane Henze, who had headed the League of Women Voters' school finance study a few years earlier, I came to understand the changes better than some school administrators did.

Come October, we knew we were gaining on Stranik. He may have known it too—especially when he looked up from comfortably watching a Minnesota Vikings game one Sunday afternoon at home to see me knocking on his door. Local journalists were hearing a buzz. WCCO-TV sent an up-and-coming female journalist, Susan Spencer, to my house early one morning to do a day-in-the-candidate's-life feature story. I had the four kids all scrubbed and shiny for breakfast when Spencer arrived, and told them that if they would be on their best behavior, we would eat at McDonald's that night. That did the trick. They spoke happily about Mom's campaign while our visitor was present. Spencer surveyed the idyllic domestic scene and incisively asked, "Are you sure it's like this every morning?"

In fact, my children were supportive of my campaign, so much so that they participated in a few summer campaign events and helped with the biggest parade of the season in my district, the one at the Hopkins Raspberry Festival. The older children ran ahead of the car in which I was riding, passing out flyers to the crowd along the parade route. Five-year-old Patrick rode in a borrowed convertible with me. He thought it was great fun until a few of his schoolmates spotted him and called out to him. Then, suddenly self-conscious, he dived to the floor of the car and stayed there for the duration. That was his last parade!

DFL bigwigs were slow to catch on to our campaign's growing strength, however, even though Hank Fischer, the state party's executive director and soon-to-be state chair, lived in my district. Finally, in late October, he dispatched a young aide named Mark Winkler to my door with an offer to help. "Great!" I said. "You babysit my kids while I go door-knocking!" I don't believe Mark ever came back—though I would see him again in the secretary of state's office a few years later.

We knew the campaign was going well. We were especially pleased to have met and recruited so many women, and liked to think that our campaign would increase turnout among women voters. Nevertheless, we didn't let ourselves believe that we would win. The odds were too long against us. As snow fell on election eve, Gretchen, Diane Henze, and I campaigned together one last time until 9 PM. We talked about what we would say the following night at the campaign party Diane and her husband, Dick, had graciously offered to host at their large home. Our volunteers had done such a superb job. I don't know how any of them could have worked harder. What would we say to them when word came that we had lost? To practice for the next evening, we tried a few lines of condolence on one of our workers who had shouldered responsibility for a whole precinct.

"It's going to be tough," we told her with soothing voices.

"No, we're going to be fine," she brightly assured. "We've counted our votes. Don't worry, we've got this. We're going to win our precinct."

Her assessment matched that of every other precinct leader on the Growe team. And they were right. We won every single precinct. We were told later that as we celebrated that night, House DFL leader and soon-to-be Speaker Martin Sabo was heard to mutter, "Joan Growe won? Who's Joan Growe?" He had never heard of me. That was about to change.

• • •

The story of my 1972 campaign has a rich epilogue. It was never "my" campaign. It was "our" campaign, and the women who waged it with me went on to lives of remarkable accomplishment and service. We started riding feminism's second wave together, and it took us to places beyond our imagining.

Gretchen Fogo enrolled in seminary and became a United Methodist minister and director of church relations at Hamline University. Nancy Wangen and Diane Henze went to graduate school and earned PhDs. Wangen became executive director of Intersystem Collaboration, a higher education consortium, and Henze became a psychologist in private practice. I can tell similar stories about other campaign workers—Elizabeth Zerby, who became a lawyer; Sonja Anderson, who became an expert on affirmative action in education; Vicki Lansky, who wrote best-selling parenting books; Arlene Nystuen, who became a lobbyist and activist for women in the criminal justice system; Janet Leslie, who became an activist in Planned Parenthood and Junior Achievement. Janet Yonehiro, who had been elected to the Minnetonka City Council in 1971, became the first female candidate for mayor in that city a few years later. Though she did not win, she paved the way for another League of Women Voters member, Karen Anderson, to serve twenty years on the city council and become Minnetonka's first female mayor in 1993.[9]

I am sometimes asked what took us so long. Why did American women born in the 1920s and 1930s wait until the 1970s to seek and seize more opportunities? The nation's good economy and the stirrings of the civil rights and antiwar movements had something to do with launching the second wave of the American women's movement, I'm sure. But for me and the other Growe campaigners, change sprang from the encouragement we gave each other. We saw talent in each other, and said so. We set ambitious goals and assured each other we could meet them. We picked each other up day after day by saying, "We can do this. We can organize, because that's what women do best. We know how to do two things at once—it's what we always do." We gave each other practical help—picking up each other's children, preparing and delivering meals, babysitting, cleaning. We acknowledged the importance of all of our roles, in and out of the home. We became close and lasting friends.

As a result, we gained a sense of empowerment—and that power animates us to this day. In fact, we still refer to ourselves as the Minnetonka Mafia.

4

Open Government

"The women are taking over!" I heard that more than once as my class of freshmen legislators was sworn into office on January 2, 1973. It was far from true. Of the 134 members of the Minnesota House, just six were women. No woman served that year in the state Senate. Only one woman, Laura Naplin, had ever occupied a seat in that chamber, and she had left office in 1934.

Yet the seating of the six of us—Helen McMillan of Austin, Linda Berglin and Phyllis Kahn of Minneapolis, Mary Forsythe of Edina, Ernee McArthur of Brooklyn Center, and me—constituted a breakthrough. Only Helen had served in 1971. In 1972, forty-three female candidates campaigned for legislative office, far more than in any previous year. That surge was the result of a concerted effort by organizations as old as the League of Women Voters, conceived in 1919, and as new as the Minnesota Women's Political Caucus, founded in 1971. It was no fluke or fad. The number of women in the legislature would increase in each of the next dozen elections.[1]

While our numbers were small in 1973, they were more than the House was prepared for. I discovered as much on my second day in office, during a prolonged floor debate over House rules. A "call of the House" had been issued that required all members to remain on the floor or in the adjacent retiring room and offices so that members would be on hand to cast imminently expected votes. A call of the House meant no physical discomfort for male legislators. A toilet to serve them was adjacent to the retiring room, right off the chamber. But no ladies' room was close at hand. We women had to leave the chamber and walk through the crowd of lobbyists and visitors that congregated outside to get to the nearest bathroom, and then stand in line behind twenty second graders. What's more, during a call of the House, we were obliged to wave our hands and get the permission of the House Speaker to leave. When I was compelled to do that on my second day in office, I felt as if I was back in grade school.

A few weeks later, I related that demeaning experience to *Minneapolis Star* reporter Peter Vaughan, who reported it prominently in a column about how we women were faring in the "men's club" that the legislature had long been. I gave him more evidence of the institution's male orientation: legislators' identification badges, designed to fit in the breast pocket of a man's suit; the microphones with clips to attach to a man's lapel; the invitation I had received to join the Dome Club, an organization of legislators' wives. But I also acknowledged that being among the few females in a male-dominated institution gave me the advantage of visibility, including the kind of media attention that Vaughan's column represented.[2]

I set out to put that advantage to good use in my first speech during a House floor debate. It was on a matter about which I felt very strongly then, and still do: adding a guarantee of gender equality under the law to the US Constitution via the Equal Rights Amendment (ERA). It galls me that women still lack an explicit guarantee of equal standing with men in this nation's foundational charter. Early in the 1973 session, Minnesota became the twenty-sixth state to ratify the ERA. By 1977, thirty-five states had ratified the amendment, three fewer than needed to put it into the Constitution. Two more ratified in 2017 and 2018, and in January 2020, Virginia joined them. It will now go to the courts to determine whether a 1982 ratification deadline imposed by Congress is valid. If that deadline falls, victory will finally have come in a ratification quest that began in March 1972.[3]

The Minnesota House's ratification debate and vote fell by fateful coincidence on January 22, 1973, just hours after the US Supreme Court legalized abortion in the first two trimesters of pregnancy and tossed a grenade into American politics. I made no mention of that very fresh decision when I rose to speak on the House floor. Rather, I stressed that 42 percent of all adult American women were in the workforce. (Today, the share is 57 percent.) Those working women deserve the assurance of equal access to education and unbiased treatment in the workplace that the ERA would provide, I said. I also addressed opponents' claims that the ERA would somehow be detrimental to women who did not work outside their homes. "Raising a family is a joint responsibility where a husband and wife should share equally the joys and burdens and make equal contributions. This is a private acceptance of responsibility on the part of husband and wife. The Equal Rights Amendment can neither prevent nor enforce such mutual acceptance. We must stop the myth-making and face reality."[4]

To my delight, the Minnesota House's ratification vote that day was 104–28. As is the House's custom, I was the recipient of a blizzard of handwritten notes from my political peers about my "maiden" speech, some sincere, some snarky. "For a woman, I thought you did an excellent job," wrote state representative Joe Graba of Wadena. Even the governor weighed in: "Joan—That was a terrific speech. Would you consider giving the governor's next joint session speech? Wendy."

The presence of more women was just one of the changes that made the 1973 session a watershed for the Minnesota Legislature. That year also brought the seating of the first two African American legislators in the twentieth century, Ray O. Pleasant of Bloomington and B. Robert Lewis of St. Louis Park. It marked the return of annual sessions, a first since the switch to biennial sessions in 1879. The change had come via a constitutional amendment approved by the voters in 1972. It allowed the legislature to recess rather than adjourn on the Monday after the third Saturday in May of odd-numbered years and reconvene on a date of its choice in subsequent even-numbered years.[5]

More significantly, 1973 brought Minnesota all-DFL control of state government for the first time. Voters gave DFLers a 37–30 majority in the state Senate, ending 114 years of Conservative Caucus (Republican) control in that chamber. DFLers would keep their hold on the Senate for the next thirty-eight years. With the House at seventy-seven DFLers and fifty-seven Republicans and DFL governor

Wendell Anderson in the state capitol's executive suite, DFLers were in a position to deliver on policy promises they had been making for many years.[6]

• • •

What we DFLers had at the top of our to-do list might be surprising in twenty-first-century eyes. We weren't pursuing more spending, higher taxes, or social justice guarantees—not as our marquee issues, anyway. Rather, we were promoting changes in elections and law-making procedures intended to give citizens more control of government. It's what many of us had campaigned on in 1972. Our mantra was that Minnesotans deserved "openness in government." End the secrecy, we argued, and the result would be greater accountability, less self-dealing—something Minnesotans abhor in politics—and, ultimately, better policy.

Openness proved to be both a potent and a politically convenient issue in the 1972 election, for a variety of reasons. It united DFLers, whose roots in both the Democratic Party of the nineteenth century and the populist Farmer-Labor Party of the early twentieth century favored the empowerment of average people over plutocrats. Encouraging citizen participation in Minnesota government was part of the DFL's institutional DNA. My party held that more citizen involvement would make government a better tool for solving the shared problems of common folk.

For DFLers, talking about state and local government operations also nicely diverted attention from the weakness of Senator George McGovern's presidential candidacy and the liberal tilt of the state DFL's 1972 platform. It had been adopted during the state party convention's waning hours, when many more conservative Greater Minnesota delegates had already departed. It endorsed same-sex marriage forty-one years before Minnesota state law would finally follow suit. It also favored legalization of recreational marijuana use (an issue still being debated in 2020) and conditional amnesty for draft dodgers. Plenty of DFLers, Governor Anderson among them, felt compelled to disavow that platform, then change the subject as quickly as they could.[7]

The openness issue also played well in the wake of the performance of the 1971 legislature. Republican majorities that year finally delivered major changes in state tax and education finance policy after what remains the longest special session in state history. It didn't end until October 30 that year—more than five months after the regular session expired—and it made most of its major decisions in private, leadership-only huddles that even other legislators, let alone journalists or citizens, were not allowed to attend. That prolonged secrecy irritated Minnesotans, especially as DFLers reminded voters that House Republicans (conservatives) had spurned the minority's attempts to require that legislative meetings be open and recorded, and that votes be publicly tallied. DFLers in the House had also tried to require disclosure of legislators' personal financial interests, suspecting that some were too cozy with special interests. That was remembered in April 1972, when reports surfaced that business lobbying groups were funneling tens of thousands of undisclosed dollars to the House conservative caucus and, it was alleged, into the hands of one unelected GOP political operative. Control of those funds became a matter of hot intracaucus dispute that spilled into the headlines. When the Watergate scandal erupted in Washington in June 1972, Minnesotans had more reason to link Republicans with surreptitious and potentially nefarious political activity.[8]

That was the backdrop of Governor Anderson's 1973 annual State of the State message, which spelled out the DFL's openness-in-government agenda on the second day of the new session. "It is our unique mandate to extend the spirit and energy of reform to government itself," Anderson said. He briefly acknowledged a connection between the election of more women and government reform. "No other session has had as many women members," he said. "This newness, this freshness provides us with a special opportunity to demonstrate to the people of Minnesota that government works, and it works for them."[9]

Anderson's "openness" wish list included a return to party designation in legislative races (to remove the "blindfolds in the voting booth," as the governor put it); public financing of political campaigns through a voluntary tax-return checkoff system; campaign donation disclosure requirements; the creation of more citizen-based public policy boards and commissions to advise or direct state agencies; redistricting via a bipartisan commission rather than legislators themselves; and direct election of the members of the Metropolitan Council. All but the last two of those proposals would become law.

So would two others that figure in my story: an extension of the 1957 Minnesota Open Meeting Law to much of state government and all local governments; and the creation of a statewide voter-registration system that included an opportunity to register to vote on Election Day.

• • •

When the Minnesota Newspaper Association approached me about being the chief sponsor of a bill to require more local governments to conduct their business in open meetings, I jumped at the chance. Minnesota passed its first open meeting law for local governments in 1957. But it included no penalty for violation, and it omitted both state agencies and the committees and subcommittees of local governments. I had seen in Minnetonka how easy it was for local government officials to evade the law. A few weeks after Janet Yonehiro was seated as the only woman on the city council in 1971, I asked her how it was going.[10]

"It's pretty frustrating," she said. "I get to the council meeting and see an item on the agenda, and I discover that it's already been decided. We don't discuss it at all." I went to the next council meeting to see for myself the open meeting charade that was being performed. I found it offensive, so much so that I asked Janet to join me after the meeting. We set off, following the cars of the male council members as they left city hall. We watched as they all entered a local beer-and-pizza joint. This is where the real meeting happens, we surmised. After the next meeting, we vowed, we'll be ready for them.

We set off for the pizza place promptly after the next meeting, so we were inconspicuously seated and watching when the male members of the council arrived and gathered at a table. As they began to discuss city business, we popped up and crashed their party. "Hi, guys! You didn't let me know we were having a meeting," Janet said as we approached their table. "So this is where the meeting happens!"

In that setting and with me standing by paying witness, they didn't dare refuse her a seat at the table. After that, there were no more Minnetonka City Council pizza-parlor meetings.

Such conduct was then commonplace among Minnesota elected officials, including legislators. A few days before the session started, Helen McMillan kindly agreed to have dinner with Gretchen Fogo and me. Gretchen, my campaign's comanager, was joining me at the capitol to coordinate a steady stream of volunteers—many of the same women who had worked on my campaign—who agreed to help me stay abreast of legislative issues and connected with constituents. Helen, then starting her sixth term in the House, met us at the venerable St. Paul Hotel, a downtown institution that in those years was the weeknight home for a number of Greater Minnesota legislators when the legislature was in session. We sat at the hotel's bar and watched with wide eyes as Helen spotted and named her fellow legislators as they came and went. "This is where all the decisions are made," she said, with the dismay of a former state League of Women Voters president audible in her voice.[11]

To my regret, my bill did not impose a statutory open meeting requirement on the legislature itself. It likely would not have advanced far through the legislature's committee process if it had. Legislators habitually prefer using the institution's internal rules, not statutes, to govern their own operating procedures. On the first day of the session, proposed changes in House rules to require more open doors were presented to the House DFL Steering Committee, where I was a new member.

"This will pass, won't it?" I asked Irv Anderson, the wily DFL majority leader from International Falls. "Why wouldn't everyone vote for this?" After all, I said, we had all campaigned on a promise to open government to public view, and the DFL state platform had specified as much.

His terse response and tight smile taught me a lesson about the institution I'd joined. "Joan, that was the party," Anderson said. "This is the caucus. Two different things."

We DFL freshmen didn't give in—and to our happy surprise, we largely prevailed. House rules were changed to allow minority representation on the Rules Committee for the first time—something Martin Sabo had sought without success as minority leader in 1971. We also required that all committee activity be conducted in public, and proceedings and votes in committee meetings and on the House floor be recorded for public inspection. Those were sea changes in legislative processes that would have far-reaching effects.[12]

While the legislature itself went unmentioned, my bill extended the state's 1957 open meeting law to every other state and local government entity that "transacted public business in a meeting." The 1957 law had been vague enough to allow committees, agencies, and other panels of elected officials to escape the requirement that the public must be allowed in. My bill also added a civil penalty for violations, ranging from a $100 fine to expulsion from office. Narrow exceptions were spelled out for the state Board of Pardons, the state's adult and youth corrections commissions, and other quasi-judicial panels dealing with employee discipline. My bill was not popular with the League of Minnesota Cities and the Association of Minnesota Counties, which tend to resist any new state mandates on local operations. But it was a part of the DFL's openness agenda that quite a few Republicans could support. I got the bill through the House on a 102–16 vote. The bill's Senate sponsor, Hubert H. "Skip" Humphrey III—who like me was serving his first term—worried that he would have a harder time. But the Senate vote was a solid 46–16. The open meeting bill was the most important one I sponsored during my brief legislative tenure. I am convinced that Minnesota's openness requirement has prevented a great deal of the mischief and misconduct that have eroded trust in government in other states.[13]

• • •

I had comparatively little involvement with the 1973 bill that would have an even bigger effect on Minnesota democracy and, eventually, on me: the voter registration bill. It included Election Day (also called same-day) registration, a feature that has proven effective at increasing voter turnout in each of the states that have employed it to date. Yet it faced considerable Republican hostility then, and still meets with GOP resistance today.[14]

Voter registration has an antidemocratic history in America. It arose in the nineteenth century along with residency requirements as a tactic to deny the vote to the immigrants who were then arriving to join the workforce of a rapidly industrializing nation. Later, registration requirements were among the voting barriers constructed in the Deep South to foil the Fifteenth Amendment to the US Constitution, ratified in 1870. That amendment aimed to extend the electoral franchise to African Americans, but it did not outlaw barriers to registration and voting based on property ownership, literacy, or payment of poll taxes. Those onerous requirements intentionally targeted people of color. That history may explain why North Dakota—a state heavily populated by northern European immigrants in the twentieth century—dropped a voter registration requirement for state and federal elections in 1951. Today it is the only US state that does not register voters, though it does require voters to present proof of identification at the polls.[15]

Minnesota also had no statewide voter registration system prior to 1973, likely for the same reasons. But beginning in 1959, the legislature required voter registration in Minnesota cities with populations greater than ten thousand. That policy appeared to be grounded in a presumption that urban election judges were less likely to know voters personally compared with those in small towns and rural areas and would therefore be less able to notice a nonresident or ineligible would-be voter. The city-only registration requirement meant that in the 1972 election, three out of five eligible Minnesotans were obliged to register with their county election authorities at least twenty days before an election in order to vote. The effect was to disenfranchise far too many urban voters.[16]

In his State of the State address, Governor Anderson decried that downside. "In the 1972 campaign in Minnesota, several hundred thousand potential voters failed to register, in spite of a vigorous bipartisan registration effort," Anderson said. He wasn't complaining about the election's result. Voters had been good to the DFL in 1972 despite Republican president Richard Nixon's thumping of Democratic challenger George McGovern. Rather, I suspect, he was comparing voter turnout in Minnesota in the 1950s, prior to the registration requirement in larger cities, to that in 1972. It was a substantial difference—77 percent in 1952 and 83 percent in 1956, compared with just 70 percent in 1972. Many factors other than registration likely contributed to that difference, including voter antipathy for both presidential candidates in 1972 and the swelling young-adult population in the late 1960s and early 1970s. Then and now, young adults are less likely than their elders to vote. Still, it was a troubling trend.[17]

"This legislature must give serious consideration to a system which permits a voter to register on election day if he has not already done so," Anderson said. He then added a line that I would utter myself countless times in coming decades: "Voting is a right, and not a privilege."

That's a powerful assertion that has been controversial throughout American history. Arguments about who should be allowed to vote are as old as the nation itself. I side with those who maintain that universal suffrage for adult citizens, regardless of class, race, or gender, is mandated by this nation's founding principles, starting with the Declaration of Independence. It's also consistent with Minnesota's strong tradition of participatory democracy, seen in the state's embrace of voting rights for African Americans more than a year before the Fifteenth Amendment was ratified. (Less to Minnesota's credit: that same 1868 state constitutional amendment limited Native American voting to those "who have adopted the language, customs and habits of civilization," as determined by a judge.)[18]

If one believes voting is a right, it follows that few if any circumstances should disqualify a citizen from eligibility to vote. Screening requirements that work to deny eligible people access to the polls are unacceptable. Election policies should aim to facilitate voting, not impede it. And election administrators are obliged to provide reasonably convenient voting procedures for all voters, not just the middle-class, able-bodied majority.

Needlessly complex voter registration requirements were under political fire in the early 1970s. The civil rights movement of the previous decade had called attention to the issue as it pushed into law the 1965 Voting Rights Act. That landmark legislation outlawed the barriers to African American voting that sprang up in the former Confederacy after slavery ended. It's likely no coincidence that the first states to put easier voter registration on their 1973 legislative agendas were Maine and Minnesota. Both states could trace their cultural heritage to the democracy-minded Puritans of the seventeenth century and antislavery Yankees in the nineteenth century.[19]

A pair of first-term legislators, Senator Steve Keefe of Minneapolis and Representative John Tomlinson of St. Paul, shepherded Minnesota's bill into law. They were approached by the governor's office to carry the voter registration bill in part because their professional backgrounds suggested that they knew how to handle complexity. Keefe was a chemist at Honeywell, Inc., in Minneapolis; Tomlinson a chemical engineer at 3M in suburban St. Paul. They told the capitol press corps that, initially, they both had been skeptical about Election Day registration. But "exhaustive study" had convinced them that the approach their bill prescribed included measures that would suffice to keep elections free of fraud. As the *Minneapolis Tribune* reported, "The bill requires anyone registering on election day to produce a driver's license bearing an address in the precinct, or a witness who is already registered. That is more than present registration procedures require, [Keefe and Tomlinson] noted." Stiff penalties for anyone caught voting in more than one precinct would deter fraud, they argued. So would the creation of Minnesota's first uniform voter registration lists, to be maintained according to exacting standards by each of the state's eighty-seven counties and made available to the public.[20]

Republicans disagreed. Election Day registration would be "a clearcut invitation to corruption," the bill's GOP critics told reporters. They conjured implausible claims about busloads of vagrant voters, moving from polling place to polling place on Election Day to cast multiple ballots and/or claiming identities drawn at random from graveyards and telephone directories. In their telling, all of these fraudsters would vote Democratic, under the orders of Boss Kelm, a reference to Governor Wendell Anderson's chief of staff, Tom Kelm. DFLers were pressing for easier voting to perpetuate their newfound legislative majorities, Republicans charged.[21]

That argument didn't wash with the editorial writers at the state's largest newspaper, the *Minneapolis Tribune,* which endorsed Election Day registration along with other features of the bill. Those included the ability for voters to preregister via postcard, something that Minnesota's US senators Hubert Humphrey and Walter Mondale were then promoting at the national level. The editorial envisioned the opportunity for postcard preregistration becoming so easy and ubiquitous that almost no one would register on Election Day. About that, however, the editorial was wrong. In several state general elections since 2000, the share of voters registering on Election Day has topped 18 percent.[22]

The voter registration bill passed on near party-line votes: 36–28 in the Senate on May 10, and 77–42 in the House on May 17. Anderson signed it into law on May 24. I'm not sure we were aware at the time that a similar measure was moving toward enactment in Maine. There, Democratic governor Kenneth Curtis signed Election Day registration into law on May 25. Minnesota had achieved first-in-the-nation bragging rights by a single day.[23]

I played no special role in the voter registration bill, other than eagerly casting my vote with the majority. But I took note of the fact that Minnesota's chief election administrator, Republican secretary of state Arlen Erdahl, opposed it. On the day the House sent the bill to Anderson, Erdahl publicly called on the DFL governor to veto it. "Erdahl said the bill raises the possibility of fraudulent voting as well as congestion in polling places caused by late-registering voters," the *Minneapolis Star* reported. I made a mental note of the difference in our thinking. I considered high turnout at the polls a good thing. Minnesota of all states should not have a chief election officer who would think otherwise, I said to myself.[24]

I would soon be making that point to anyone who would listen.

5

Chief Election Officer

Arlen Erdahl was forty-two years old in 1973 and did not seem to be a man in love with his job. A farmer from Blue Earth, near the Iowa border, Erdahl had been a Republican legislator for eight years, had worked in Washington for Michigan US representative Gerald Ford (the future president) and Oregon senator Mark Hatfield, and had earned a master's degree in public administration from Harvard University before running for secretary of state in 1970. Erdahl had been one of the so-called Young Turk Republicans in the Minnesota House, a name the pundits bestowed on the philosophically moderate pragmatists who rose into prominence in the Minnesota Republican Party in the 1960s. I'd guess that when he ran for secretary of state, he had expected to serve alongside another Young Turk, Governor Doug Head, and to play a prominent role in enacting the progressive GOP wing's agenda. Instead, Head lost the 1970 gubernatorial election and Erdahl found himself overshadowed in the state's executive branch by charismatic DFL governor Wendell Anderson. His Republican counterparts in state office were two staid functionaries, State Auditor Rolland Hatfield and State Treasurer Val Bjornson. Together, the three of them blended into state government's background.[1]

I seldom saw Erdahl at the capitol when I was a legislator. I later heard from a number of county auditors—the local officials with whom the secretary of state must work closely to administer elections—that they, too, had little contact with him. I knew he didn't like the new law bringing voter registration to parts of the state that had not required it before and allowing voters to register on Election Day.

It was a law I strongly supported. I began to wonder whether Erdahl would seek a second term—and whether I should try to wrest the secretary of state's office from him if he did.

Then on the day after Christmas, two announcements came from the Republican ranks. First, Ancher Nelsen, an eight-term representative serving Minnesota's south-central Second Congressional District, announced that he would not seek a ninth term in 1974. Erdahl immediately announced his intention to run for Nelsen's seat. Second, the same edition of the *St. Cloud Times* that reported Erdahl's news also announced that St. Cloud's DFL mayor Al Loehr, previously thought to be considering a congressional bid, was now likely to run for secretary of state. So were two male DFL state senators, Win Borden of Brainerd and David Schaaf of Fridley.[2]

No mention was made of me or any other possible female candidates. That may be because through the first 115 years of state history, no woman had been elected to any Minnesota statewide office in her own right. That phrase makes allowance for the fact that some women—specifically widows—had been appointed to elective offices to complete the unfinished terms of their deceased husbands. That was how the one and only woman to hold statewide office prior to 1973 initially landed her job. Coincidentally, her office was secretary of state. "Mrs. Mike Holm" was on the 1952 ballot. Virginia Paul Holm had chosen that version of her name to advertise to voters that she was the widow of Republican secretary of state Mike Holm, whom Minnesotans had unfailingly elected to that office every two years between 1920 and his death on July 6, 1952. (State officials served two-year terms prior to 1962.) Her DFL opponent took her to court in an attempt to compel her to put her given name, Virginia, on the ballot in place of "Mrs. Mike." A court ruled that the suit had been filed too late to be considered. DFLers had to wait until 1954 to oust Virginia, er, "Mrs. Mike," from the office.[3]

The 1954 winner, Joseph Donovan, was the only DFLer or Democrat since 1860 to serve as secretary of state. With Erdahl's ten thousand–vote margin of victory in the 1970 election, the office had reverted to Republican hands. Minnesota voters were slow to break a long habit of choosing the Republican option for low-profile offices about which they had little knowledge. But this was 1973–74, and that predilection was changing. The reason: Watergate. The political burglary and cover-up scandal that was engulfing President Richard Nixon was damaging the Republican brand name in Minnesota and around the country. I thought 1974 would be a good year for a DFLer to run for statewide office, and that my League of Women Voters work had prepared me well to serve as the state's chief election officer. It was a position in which I believed I could accomplish a great deal, perhaps more than I could as a legislator. My interest in making representative democracy work was genuine and deep.[4]

Several additional factors affected my thinking about my political future in late 1973. One pertained to a change the legislature made at Anderson's urging: putting party labels on legislative ballots. I was a DFLer who had won a nonpartisan election in 1972 in a district that otherwise routinely elected Republicans. Not having *DFL* next to my name on the ballot that year had served me well. I was confident that I could win a second term, but putting that label next to my name on the 1974 ballot would not make my reelection easier.

In addition, my victory had come because of the extraordinary door-to-door canvassing of a cadre of very able women. Those women were still my friends and supporters; several dozen had done brief volunteer stints in my legislative office. But a number of them had begun to pursue other opportunities, taking jobs or going to school to prepare for new careers. For example, my stalwart friend and campaign cochair, Gretchen Fogo, had enrolled in seminary and was on her way to becoming a United Methodist minister. I would have to rebuild my campaign team in order to run for a second term. And I would likely face a much more motivated Republican opponent.

Another factor was personal. My marriage to Glen Growe was not a happy one. I was ready for divorce. That meant I would need to return to full-time employment. My $8,400 annual legislative salary would not adequately support me and my four children, three of whom were teenagers with college on the horizon. I was prepared to return to teaching or look for other work in the private sector. But trying first for a job I knew I would enjoy in the public sector seemed like a good option. I announced my candidacy for secretary of state on January 15, 1974. Rather than run for the office himself, Dave Schaaf agreed to be my campaign manager, and Win Borden opted not to run. My only rival for the DFL Party's endorsement for the office would be Al Loehr, the St. Cloud mayor whose credentials also included work as a Department of Veterans Affairs official in the administration of DFL governor Karl Rolvaag.[5]

I was making a bigger political leap than I initially realized. With just a year as a legislator to my credit, I did not yet have a large reliable network of acquaintances and friends throughout the state. But my legislative run had shown me the value of grassroots organizing and personal campaigning. I set out to win DFL endorsement by recruiting volunteer campaign leaders in each of the state's sixty-seven state Senate districts, and making plans to visit as many of those districts as possible before the June 14–15 state convention in Minneapolis. Fortunately—thanks to rules changes in the national Democratic Party engineered in part by Minnesota US representative Don Fraser—women were participating in DFL politics in greater numbers in 1974, knowing that the state party would need to select enough women delegates to be "in reasonable relationship to their presence in the population of the state." That meant the 1974 state convention would be half female. Many of those female delegates were interested in putting a woman on the state ticket.[6]

When my campaign was still new, some prominent DFLers told me I would be well advised to ask the governor's permission before proceeding. I thought it was an odd suggestion. Yes, governors are at or near the top of any state political party's pecking order. But a governor is not granted the power to dictate who runs for other offices. The secretary of state is elected separately from the governor for good reason. Those who administer elections ought to be accountable to the people directly, and no one else.

I was acquainted with Governor Wendell Anderson, but no more than that. My legislative work seldom brought me into either his orbit or that of his forceful chief of staff, Tom Kelm. The thought of going to either of them as a supplicant did not seem right to me. But I conceded that I ought to show them courtesy and respect. Accordingly, I made an appointment not to ask permission to run but to announce my intention and invite Anderson's support. I was received politely, but no support was promised. I was told later that Anderson considered Arlen Erdahl a friend.

But Erdahl was not my opponent, I assured myself—until, suddenly, he was. At the Republicans' Second District congressional endorsing convention on April 27, thirty-year-old state representative Tom Hagedorn of Truman, a small town near the Iowa border, surprised Erdahl and most other outside observers with enough strength and staying power to win endorsement on the twentieth ballot for the open US House seat. Hagedorn was a telegenic farmer who had served just two terms in the Minnesota House. (He is the father of US representative Jim Hagedorn of Minnesota's First District, elected in 2018.) He was seen as more loyal than Erdahl to President Richard Nixon, which evidently was in keeping with the defensive mood among GOP insiders that spring. Within days of this endorsement defeat, Erdahl was back in the running for secretary of state. The other Republican candidate for that office, former Minneapolis mayor Charlie Stenvig, stepped aside to allow the incumbent to try for a second term.[7]

Erdahl's antipathy for the new voter registration law made me speak in favor of it all the more, particularly among the DFLers who had seen the political success that came with the party's 1972 theme of openness in government. How could government be open to the people if the polls were closed to those who had not preregistered? And how could a secretary of state who disliked a new registration regime implement it properly? That argument was at the heart of the speeches I made at DFL meetings and congressional district conventions that spring. Al Loehr was generally at the conventions too, touting his longer tenure in public service.

One of the first signs that delegates were moving in my direction came at the Seventh District convention in East Grand Forks. I had asked state senator Roger Moe, a popular future Senate majority leader, to introduce me that day. He was initially willing, but then he took me aside to tell me that the longtime DFL Seventh District chair, Henry Tweten, wanted to do the honors instead. Henry was the

Speaking at a political gathering, July 1974

DFL's kingmaker in that part of the state. His introduction was the equivalent of him placing a crown on my head. He told the assembled DFL faithful that he thought it was time to put a woman on the state ticket, and that he appreciated that I was what he called a "good Catholic and a regular person." I tried to say nothing that would give those delegates a contrary impression!

I was optimistic but nervous as Gloria Griffin—the future founder of the Minnesota Women's Consortium—drove me to Minneapolis for the state DFL convention. It was the first state political convention I had ever attended. I was determined to not let my inexperience show—much, anyway. I was pleased when, on the convention's eve, the *Minneapolis Star* reported that I was deemed the favorite for endorsement for secretary of state—and that Loehr was expected to seek endorsement for state auditor instead. That's exactly what happened. Propelled by support from female delegates, I was endorsed by a lopsided 798–367 vote. With TV cameras rolling, Loehr promptly announced his candidacy for auditor. He was endorsed for that post.[8]

• • •

With strong convention backing, I hoped to avoid attracting an opponent in the DFL primary, set for September 10. But I was evidently viewed as an easy target by at least one ambitious if little-known would-be politician. Richard Noonan was an electrical contractor from Bloomington who had never won state office. But he had run for secretary of state in the 1970 DFL primary. In that five-way race, he had finished dead last, winning just thirty-two thousand votes. He evidently thought his chances would be better in a two-way primary against a female candidate. Fearing that he might be right, I got busy.[9]

Tom Kelm, who was Governor Anderson's chief political agent as well as chief of staff, rented a suite of offices across from popular Peter's Grill in downtown Minneapolis and offered low-cost space and support services to all of the DFL-endorsed statewide candidates. I accepted, but resolved to spend very little time there. My dad may actually have been there more than I was. In those years, Mom and Dad came to Minneapolis to shop about once a week. Dad would come in and pick up a stack of campaign flyers and walk up and down Nicollet Mall, stopping people with a friendly greeting and an outstretched flyer. "Hi, I'm Art Anderson and my daughter is Joan Growe. I hope you vote for her," he said over and over. I suspect that I was the first and only Democrat for whom Dad ever voted.

My campaign didn't have much money, and I lacked state-level fundraising experience. But I intended to make up for those deficiencies with intense personal campaigning. Instead of going door-to-door, as I did in 1972 in Minnetonka and Eden Prairie, I would go town-to-town, always by car. Often, I was driven by the young Augsburg College graduate who had been an intern in my legislative office, Ted Grindal. (He would go on to become a leading state capitol lobbyist and a partner in the law firm Lockridge Grindal Nauen in Minneapolis.)

We set out to visit all of Minnesota's eighty-seven counties. Our days were jam-packed with stops, often so tightly scheduled that we resolved to not drink water in the car, lest an unplanned bathroom break would put us behind schedule. Our visits were usually arranged by the same county-level volunteers who had helped me win DFL endorsement. Sometimes those volunteers would gather a small group at a coffee shop or community center, where I could give a brief speech and answer questions. I would talk about my view that citizens have a right to vote—it's not something that government gives them—and that the role of the secretary of state was to make voting as easy as possible.

If the town was a county seat, I always stopped at the courthouse to meet the county auditor, whose job included election administration. "I'm planning to win this election," I would say as I introduced myself. "How can I help you?" Often, he or she would invite everyone in the office to assemble. I made a point of reassuring them about the new voter registration law. My message was that I would do all I could to help them implement it. We would be in this together.

I stopped at every local newspaper office and radio station, armed with a news release and a Polaroid camera with which to take a picture that newspapers could publish of me chatting with local people. These small enterprises were hungry for local news, and the visit of the only woman running for statewide office that year was news enough for them. Radio stations would often immediately usher me into their broadcast studios and put me on the air. But the novelty of my gender led to personal questions: Are you married? What does your husband think of your candidacy? Do you have children? Where are your children? Who's caring for them? I was well aware that the DFL's male candidates were not being asked such questions. In hopes of redirecting the conversation, I took to delivering a fact sheet about myself and the work of the secretary of state's office that included guidance for reporters, such as, "You might want to ask Joan about elections."

When I was pressed about family life, I explained that my three older children were teenagers, sufficiently self-reliant and responsible enough to babysit for other people's children. As for Patrick, who was seven in 1974, his father, Glen, was on hand, and I was lucky to find a college student whose class schedule allowed her to come to our home as needed in the late afternoon, mind Patrick after school, and start supper. My friends kindly took my turn as a carpool driver and were willing to offer more help in a pinch. It took some organizing, but home life stayed manageable.

I had prepared small posters, sized for placement in storefront windows. Those posters taught me something about regional differences in the way Minnesotans practice politics. On the heavily DFL-leaning Iron Range, store owners welcomed me and said yes without hesitation when I asked to put a poster in their windows. In southern Minnesota, which had been a Republican bastion for much of the first one hundred years of statehood, shopkeepers wanted to keep partisan politics away from their enterprises. When in that part of the state, I learned to keep my posters in the trunk of the car.

The local DFL activists who helped arrange our visits often hosted us overnight, or found someone else who could. Our campaign could not afford hotel lodging. Staying in people's homes may not have been ideally restful—I once had to sleep in a bed with two small children—but it built lasting bonds of friendship. Years later, people would approach me with outstretched arms and say, "You slept at my house!" When our overnight hosts offered to buy us dinner or asked us to join them for supper at home, we gladly accepted and became better acquainted over the meal. When farmers who had a gasoline tank on their property offered to fill up our car the next morning, we gratefully accepted. Often, we were on our way early for a breakfast meeting with voters in the next town. In the car, as someone else drove, I'd write personal thank-you notes to the people who hosted and met with us, as well as any shopkeepers who allowed us to place posters in their windows. Finding a post office to get those notes promptly mailed was part of the daily routine.

It was old-style, grassroots campaigning, employed mostly because I thought it was the only kind of campaign I could afford. In hindsight, I see other good reasons for candidates to stump the state the way I did. I encouraged everyone I met to get involved in my campaign and in politics in general, making it seem easy and worthwhile. I assured them by my presence that if they would elect me, elections would be administered by an approachable person, someone who knew and cared about them. I invited them to trust me and, by extension, to trust their government. Trust is a crucial ingredient in representative democracy, and it has seriously eroded in the past several decades. I'm convinced that if campaigns relied less on paid media attacks and more on meet-and-greet, personal campaigning, America would see a rebound in trust in government.

I don't remember running into Richard Noonan at any point during that summer's primary campaign. We did not face off in any debates. If he did any advertising, I wasn't aware of it. Yet despite his low profile, the primary election was a squeaker. I won by just fourteen thousand votes out of about three hundred thousand cast. "The narrow victory of Mrs. Growe, who may have campaigned harder than any other candidate, apparently corroborated her fear that being a woman would cost her votes," reported Joe Blade of the *Minneapolis Star* the day after the primary. It could have been worse. Two other DFL-endorsed candidates were defeated in that election. Tony Perpich, the brother of then–lieutenant governor Rudy Perpich, lost his bid for the DFL's Eighth District congressional nomination to James Oberstar, the chief of staff for retiring US representative John Blatnik. And Al Loehr was drubbed by Robert Mattson Jr., the son of a former state attorney general with the same name, in his quest for nomination for state auditor. Both Mattson and Oberstar would figure in my story ten years later.[10]

• • •

For the remainder of the 1974 campaign, my focus was unseating Arlen Erdahl. Our disagreements over election policies were real. But we had become friendly rivals. He is a gracious man with a genuine commitment to public service. Our teenaged children had become acquainted at the state fair. Both of us had dispatched our kids to perform campaign chores at the fair in exchange for spending money for food and rides. I convinced my older kids to walk around the fairgrounds wearing homemade sandwich boards advertising my candidacy; his five kids did something similar. Arlen and I laughed as we compared notes on blending politics and parenthood. I began to think it was a shame that the Republican Party had rejected his bid to be a congressman. (Four years later, when Erdahl ran for an open congressional seat in the First District, his party and the voters were more receptive. He would serve two terms in the US House.)

I kept up a full-throttle pace after the primary, with increasing optimism about the outcome. Richard Nixon resigned from the presidency in disgrace on August 9, 1974; a month later, his successor, Republican president Gerald Ford, gave Nixon a full pardon from any criminal prosecution in connection with the Watergate break-in and cover-up. Voter outrage with Republicans was palpable. It was a good time to be a Democrat running for office.

Much as I emphasized policy matters, media coverage still focused on my gender. "She's the only woman on the state ticket of either major party," Gerry Nelson of the Associated Press wrote in October in a feature story published in a number of Minnesota newspapers. Nelson, the respected dean of the capitol press corps, told readers that I wanted to increase voter turnout, require training for local election officials, and publish and distribute a state voters' guide containing information about candidates for state offices. But he also mentioned that when I campaigned, I wore "trim-cut suits and tailored dresses at a fashionable below-the-knee length." I don't think any other candidate's wardrobe got that much notice.[11]

State capitol reporters were also increasingly fixated on the abortion issue in the year after the *Roe v. Wade* decision legalized abortion. Abortion has nothing whatsoever to do with the work of the Minnesota secretary of state. But that did not deter *Minneapolis Tribune* reporter Steven Dornfeld from devoting half of a lengthy story on my race to that hot-button issue. Erdahl said he favored a constitutional amendment banning the procedure. I did not—but as a legislator, I had supported a bill that would have prohibited abortion after twenty-two weeks of pregnancy, except to protect the life or health of the mother. When on April 12, 1973, the legislature took up a bill memorializing Congress to approve the so-called Human Life Amendment to the US Constitution, I considered that a move too far. Rather than vote yes or no, I abstained. "We are faced with voting for a resolution on one hand which will make a mother who has an abortion subject to severe punishment, or voting against the resolution, which would appear to give sanction to abortion on demand. I cannot—I will not—choose between these extremes," I explained that day. I had alerted the two most prominent DFL abortion rights lobbyists, Koryne Horbal and Jeri Rasmussen, about my intentions, and thought I had their assurance that my approach was acceptable to them.[12]

Nevertheless, I paid a political price for following my conscience that day. Leaders of neither the new DFL Feminist Caucus nor the anti-abortion Minnesota Citizens Concerned for Life would support me. Horbal, the DFL Feminist Caucus coordinator, told Dornfeld that my unwillingness to complete her group's questionnaire was behind her group's nonendorsement. "I don't question that Joan Growe has ability. But we are in the business of furthering causes that are of concern to us," she said. I knew that there was more to that group's unhappiness with me than my failure to complete a questionnaire. Horbal and her allies wanted me to pledge that I wouldn't support any candidate who did not favor legalized abortion. I refused. I said my intention was to support Democratic candidates and to work within the party to encourage more pro-choice candidates to run. That wasn't good enough for Koryne. My relationship with her soured. At one point, she told me that she might run against me for secretary of state. "Go ahead," I responded. She never made good on the threat—but the DFL Feminist Caucus never endorsed me thereafter.

Stories like Dornfeld's and Nelson's weren't the only ones Minnesota readers saw in the campaign's final weeks. A proposal I announced in mid-October got considerable play in newspapers in Greater Minnesota. I said I believed citizens needed an ombudsman to help them navigate through state agencies and programs when they were in need of state government's services. That ombudsman ought to be housed in the secretary of state's office, I proposed in announcing the idea, since "the ombudsman must be a highly visible and independent office," one that "stands separate from departments and agencies" that are controlled by the governor and legislature. The fact that the secretary of state's office is filled via direct election, not gubernatorial or legislative appointment, made it ideally suited for such a role, I argued. The attention that story received in newspapers as far-flung as the *Red Wing Republican Eagle*, the *Bemidji Pioneer*, and the *Marshall Messenger Independent* indicated that the idea gave me some traction.[13]

Another good sign came from the *Minneapolis Tribune*'s Minnesota Poll, considered the gold standard in state public opinion measurement. The final poll of the campaign season, published the day before the election, found me 4 percentage points ahead of Erdahl, 43–39 percent. In mid-September, the same poll had found me trailing Erdahl, 39–32 percent. Those numbers suggested that a potentially decisive share of the electorate remained undecided. But they confirmed our campaign's sense that the race had shifted in my favor.[14]

That campaign's final days were special for me because they brought me into the orbit of a Minnesota political legend, Hubert H. Humphrey. The former vice president was back in the US Senate in 1974. He was not on the ballot that year, but was still—and always— the head of the DFL Party and its most respected voice. His decision to campaign with me the weekend before the November 5 election was a thrill for me, both personally and politically. It was an affirmation of his confidence in my vote-getting potential.

Fred Gates, Humphrey's longtime aide, told me that Humphrey had been talking up my candidacy for a number of days before he joined me. "He told some church women they needed to get off their butts and vote for Joan," Gates told me. I doubt that Humphrey used precisely those words, but the message was good to hear.

Unfortunately, an early snowstorm arrived in northwestern Minnesota to foul up our air-travel plans. A scheduled stop in Alexandria had to be canceled. I badly wanted to make that stop. My race was close, and I believed a visit there would help me make headway in that part of the state. Humphrey said, "Don't worry, Joan. I'll take care of it." He grabbed a phone and started calling reporters at every news outlet in Alexandria, one at a time. His message, as I recall it: "I'm here with Joan Growe. Joan and I have been talking about the issues in your area. Joan has been working really hard, and she's attuned to the thinking in Alexandria. We can't make it there today as we had planned. But I want you to know that I strongly support Joan Growe." It was such a sweet thing for him to do, and it's a memory I cherish.

"Anderson Leads DFL Sweep" was the headline in the state's largest newspaper the day after the election. For the first time in state history, the DFL won every state constitutional office—and it expanded its majority in the Minnesota House to a record high. (The state Senate was not on the ballot in 1974.) Wendell Anderson carried all eighty-seven counties, a political feat unmatched by any Minnesota governor. I defeated Erdahl with a decisive 92,000-vote margin. That victory was sweet. But I couldn't help notice that my 641,000 votes were fewer than had been cast in 1970 for Daniel Donovan, the DFLer who lost to Erdahl that year. "It was a widespread failure of Republicans to vote, not an upsurge in support for Democratic-Farmer-Labor candidates, that defeated the Republican Party's entire Minnesota ticket for statewide office," *Minneapolis Tribune* analyst Bernie Shellum reported the next day. That told me two things: the DFL advantage in 1974 was a product of Watergate and should not be considered permanent, and a secretary of state whose aim was to increase voter turnout had ample ground to gain.[15]

6

The Traveling Secretary

Minnesota's secretary of state is often described as the state's top election administrator. That's a fairly succinct description of the job today, but it wasn't always so. That history was on my mind as I moved into my new role in January 1975. Enticing people to vote had not consistently been the office's priority. I could not expect to be guided by a lot of institutional habits or memory.

A memo by Forrest Talbott, an assistant secretary of state from 1958 to 1971, advised his successors that the main role of Minnesota's secretary of state was that of an archivist. "The continuing importance of the office of the secretary of state as an independent, constitutional, elective office rests upon its function as the preserver of the official history of the state, as contained in the enrolled acts of the Legislature, election returns, and official documents of many kinds, and abstracted in the Legislative Manual," Talbott wrote just four years before my election. "The history and proper current use of the Great Seal is also important," he added. Maybe it was to some of my predecessors—but not to me.[1]

I was also keenly aware that if I was to succeed, I would need an abundance of local goodwill. Fundamentally, elections in Minnesota are local exercises. They are run by well-motivated local people—a lot of them. On Election Day, about thirty thousand Minnesotans serve as election judges. They sign on for modest pay to put in a very long day on the job. Their work can be tedious and even boring, but it can also be peppered with dilemmas and conflicts that must be resolved with sound ad hoc judgments. Much rides on their faithful execution of their duties. Election judges are hired and trained by county

My son Michael holds the Bible as my father administers the oath of office and I become Minnesota's secretary of state, January 1975.

and city officials in ways that in 1975 could be charitably described as mixed in effectiveness and quality. I wanted to change that, but I could not act by decree. I knew I had to bring local people along.[2]

I did two smart things right away. I hired Mark Winkler as deputy secretary of state, and Mary Ann McCoy as elections director. Those two positions plus one administrative aide were the only ones in the office that were mine to fill. The rest of the office staff—initially about twenty people in all—were civil servants, not political appointees. Mark's previous experience included work as a legislative aide to a busy state senator, Win Borden of Brainerd. His job was to manage the entire office, which includes a substantial business services division. It's the government entity responsible for reviewing, approving, and filing articles of incorporation for all the businesses and nonprofit organizations operating in Minnesota. That's largely a record-keeping function, financed by modest filing fees. It serves businesses by protecting their names and brands from the encroachment of competitors and guides new entrepreneurs in establishing a unique identity for their businesses. It's important work that seldom makes headlines.

The work Mary Ann McCoy would oversee was more visible and politically sensitive. I turned to her because of both who she was and who she was not. Mary Ann was then a fifty-year-old Duluth native and Grinnell College graduate who was also past president of the Minnesota League of Women Voters. Like me, she was schooled by that organization in the importance of citizen engagement in every aspect of government. She knew how to be a leader of a large network of volunteers. She was also a former advertising copywriter and a longtime sales associate at Dayton's department stores, able to communicate effectively with the public. What she was not was a DFL activist. She had not been a player in either political party. Though I had run as a DFLer, I had assured voters that I would keep party interests out of the administration of elections. Appointing a nonpartisan elections director underscored that message.[3]

With Mark and Mary Ann in place, I could turn to my top priority: securing acceptance of the 1973 voter registration law by local election officials—the people who could make or break it. I'd heard often during the campaign from county auditors and election judges in Greater Minnesota that they considered a uniform statewide voter registration system a burden, and that they were particularly displeased with the extra work and staffing that same-day registration required. I knew that if they were unhappy, their legislators would be too, and that the 1973 law would be in jeopardy. I was willing to join them in advocating for reasonable adjustments in the new regime, but not for its overthrow.

I had hoped that the state's first experience with Election Day registration would be such a turnout-generating success that its critics would be silenced. But I had not considered what disgust with the Watergate scandal would do to voter turnout in 1974, particularly among Republicans. Almost two hundred thousand fewer Minnesotans voted in 1974 than had in 1970, the previous midterm election. The percentage of eligible voters who cast ballots slipped below

50 percent, the lowest in a general election since record keeping began in 1950 and well below the 62.4 percent turnout in 1970. Backers of same-day registration like me took heart at the large share of those voting who opted to register at the polls—24.5 percent at the September 10 primary; 20.1 percent at the November 5 general election. But a good share of those same-day registrants were rural people who lived in counties that had no previous registration system. Many rural Minnesotans who never missed an election were registering in 1974 for the first time.[4]

That's why those numbers did not add up to a strong claim that same-day registration would be a boon to turnout—though I was confident that it would be, in time. But the 1974 experience in Minnesota did nothing to invalidate an argument that would become a consistent theme of mine for the next twenty-four years: Americans deserve a voting process that's convenient, easy, and suited to the realities of modern life. That's in keeping with the notion that voting is a right, not a privilege. That's what those of us who administer elections are entrusted to provide. I sometimes drew from my own experience to make the point. I'd say that voting requirements should be designed to accommodate a single mother who must dress three young children in snowsuits and get them all on a bus to run any errand outside her immediate neighborhood.

With that theme in mind, I directed my administrative aide Sharon Wemlinger (who, ironically, was a former aide to my DFL-endorsement rival, Al Loehr) to start accepting as many speaking invitations from civic organizations and gatherings of local government officials as my time and our office budget would permit. Such invitations were arriving at a fast clip in 1975. I was seen as something of a novelty. Imagine, a woman in a state constitutional office! People wanted to see for themselves whether I was real. I wanted to continue the meetings with county auditors that I'd started while campaigning. Any summons to a Rotary Club was also an excuse for a stop at the county courthouse to talk shop about elections. I aimed to assure auditors that their secretary of state was their ally and, if need be, their troubleshooter with the legislature.

I asked the 1975 legislature to require that election judges receive several hours of standardized training and to give my office more funding to prepare training materials. Until then, training was haphazard and nonuniform, when it happened at all. I thought it would be easy for the legislators who had approved a statewide voter registration system just two years earlier to see that properly training election judges was essential to making that system work.

The legislature was again in DFL hands in 1975. In fact, Watergate had given the 1975 House its largest DFL majority before or since, 104–30. The downsized state Republican Party was so eager to distance itself from Watergate and the stain of Richard Nixon that in 1975 it renamed itself the Independent-Republican Party, a name that would last for the next twenty years.

But the post-Watergate DFL dominance did not mean that the legislature was keen to trample on local prerogatives or that government spending spigots had opened wide. The national economy had weakened in the mid-1970s, and state revenues lag whenever that happens. Legislators refused to require that election judges undergo training. But they did appropriate a modest sum for training materials. With that sum plus money I cobbled together from federal and internal sources, my office prepared a training manual for election judges and made it available to every county.

When possible, I met with clusters of county auditors and other election officials at meetings soon after the manual was delivered, to present it personally and hear their concerns. On a few such occasions, I arrived at those gatherings expecting to see a dozen or so staffers, only to be surprised by a crowd of a hundred or more people. "We invited our wives. They wanted to meet you," my hosts explained. "They've never seen a secretary of state before," one man told me. I surmised that he meant they had never seen a woman in that role before.

At one meeting, a wife in the audience had a question about voting, one I assumed she wanted answered in the presence of her husband. "When did Minnesota pass a law that allows husbands to come into the voting booth with their wives?" she asked somewhat timidly. I was happy to assure her and everyone else in the room that there was no such law. I told her she was entitled to privacy in the voting booth, and if her husband attempted to deny her that right, election judges would be on hand and trained to help her exercise it.

I didn't often hear complaints about the 1973 voter registration changes in those settings. County auditors had one same-day-registration election behind them. They had buckled down and implemented the new law. For many of them, it was a point of pride that they had done it reasonably well. But neither would they have anything positive to say about the changes. In "Minnesota Nice" fashion, they were pretty reserved.

Some of them took to the US mail after our meetings to be more vocal. For example, Dean E. Irlbeck, the county auditor in far-northern Lake of the Woods County, wrote a long letter in November 1975 disagreeing with my contention that same-day registration would be a boon to turnout. "Constant changing of laws and procedures causes confusion and difficulty to both the voter and the persons who administer elections. This is one of the major causes for low voter turnout," along with too few genuine contests on the ballot, he wrote.

When I received a letter like that, I tried to avoid an argumentative response, even when I strongly disagreed. My goal instead was to make friends and build trust. My response to Irlbeck was soothing: "I appreciated your comments regarding voter apathy and I can't disagree with your conclusions. Our problem is how to convince the voter that he does make a difference and has a responsibility to exercise his opinion at the polls. We should plan a talk session some day and have several people who are concerned just sit around and throw out ideas. I am not sure if we can come up with a perfect answer but it is worth thinking about."[5]

Those initial meetings set a pattern I would follow throughout my tenure. After each legislative session, I would prepare flip charts describing any changes in elections or corporate registration law. Then I'd schedule meetings with groups of city and township clerks and county auditors and hit the road. I would be joined by my office's elections director—first Mary Ann McCoy, then, in 1981, Grace Haukoos (the wife of a Republican legislator, helping maintain the office's reputation for partisan fairness), and after 1988, the incomparable Joe Mansky. We would aim to meet with about a third of the state's local election administrators each year. That would require about seven or eight treks to Greater Minnesota each summer and fall. We always drove to keep costs down. We could have arranged to use the state-owned plane that the governor used, but it was a larger model and required two pilots, and my office would be charged for its use. I thought it was too expensive. We tried to avoid overnight stays. When two-day trips were unavoidable, Mary Ann or Grace and I would share a room to minimize costs.[6]

I am frugal by nature. That may be one of the reasons I looked askance at the secretary of state's operating budget in 1975. I wanted to wring any waste out of existing funds so that I could improve elections without appealing to the legislature for more money. I asked the state Department of Administration to conduct what amounted to an internal audit. That study confirmed what I suspected: we could do better. For example, it said, "Responsibilities within the elections division are somewhat fragmented. No one employee has been assigned the responsibility for the proper disposition of fees generated by the special edition of the Legislative Manual, the Federal Election Report, and for inspecting voting machines. Fee deposits are made on an irregular basis."

That study taught me more than I expected to learn. Its release was handled by the Department of Administration, not my office. That was a mistake. The *Minneapolis Star* picked it up and ran with a story under the headline, "State Secretary's Office Criticized on Cash Handling." The *Star* did not report that I had actually asked for the study. The article left a distinct impression that I was guilty of sloppy financial management. That omission was made despite the study's explanation that "the secretary requested that a formal organization and management study be conducted by the Department of Administration" so that I might "expand services currently available to the general public."[7]

I hastily called capitol reporters to a next-day news conference and issued a statement explaining the origin of the study. I was angry, and it showed. "I deeply resent the incredibly erroneous statement that my office was 'taken to task' by the report, when the fact is that every function the study commented on was a carryover from my predecessor's administration of this office, and I had in fact recognized the need for change and requested a professional study to make recommendations," my release said. The next day, the *Minneapolis Star* printed a second, smaller, less visible story reporting that I had requested the study. But I feared that by then, the damage to the office's reputation was done. I learned the importance of telling my own story, good or bad, before others told it for me.[8]

• • •

The 1976 election coincided with the nation's bicentennial. Patriotism was in the air. I thought it was a good time to launch an old-fashioned get-out-the-vote campaign, Vote '76. Funded by a nonprofit consortium of businesses and nonprofits that we called the Minnesota Citizenship Fund, it featured posters drawn by notable Minnesota cartoonists and competition among cities and counties for highest turnout, most registered, and most improved turnout and registration numbers. Corny as it was, the contest idea caught on, with St. Paul mayor George Latimer challenging Minneapolis to a turnout duel. The clever images on the campaign's posters won them wide notice. One by *Minneapolis Tribune* cartoonist Richard Guindon was especially memorable. It featured a classic grandmotherly figure and pleaded, "Vote! Your mom would want you to." Years later, I often saw that poster on display in meeting rooms and election bureaus throughout the state.[9]

That get-out-the-vote campaign was one of several factors that augured in favor of a turnout surge in 1976 in Minnesota. The presence of Minnesota's own Walter Mondale on the presidential ballot as Democratic candidate Jimmy Carter's running mate was another boost. I am convinced that the opportunity to register to vote on Election Day also played a role—and editorial writers at the *Minneapolis Tribune* came to the same conclusion. More than 450,000 voters— more than one in five—registered on November 2, Election Day. Put those factors together, and 73 percent of the state's eligible adults cast ballots in 1976. While that was far from the record 83 percent turnout in 1956, it was up substantially from 1972. Minnesota led the nation in the percentage of eligible citizens who voted. It was an encouraging

Richard Guindon's poster for the Vote '76 competition

Another perspective, from November 1988, on my efforts to get out the vote. Craig MacIntosh, St. Paul Pioneer Press

result, not least because it gave me bragging points for my reelection campaign in 1978.[10]

By 1978, the Watergate backlash that had benefited Democratic candidates in Minnesota had abated. Hubert Humphrey, the DFL's revered founder, died that January, leaving behind a party that was badly divided. Governor Wendell Anderson was now US Senator Wendell Anderson, discovering that the popularity he had enjoyed as governor did not spare him from disapproval when he arranged his own appointment to Mondale's Senate seat at the end of 1976. Governor Rudy Perpich, the lieutenant governor who took Anderson's place, was tainted in some voters' minds by his role in Anderson's self-appointment scheme. Humphrey's Senate seat was also in play, and the DFL primary battle for the nomination to fill it was a brawl. It was won by DFL maverick businessman Robert Short, ending the congressional career of US representative Don Fraser from Minneapolis. As a DFLer, I had been lucky to run for statewide office for the first time in 1974. I worried that my luck could run out in 1978.

Independent-Republicans found strong candidates for the top three offices on the 1978 ballot—US representative Al Quie for governor; and prominent businessman Rudy Boschwitz and former gubernatorial chief of staff Dave Durenberger for the two US Senate seats. State representative Arne Carlson was a formidable challenger to Robert Mattson Jr. for the state auditor's job. But to my relief, the GOP was less able to recruit top-tier talent for the other offices on the ballot. For secretary of state, the party endorsed Gerald Brekke, an education professor at Gustavus Adolphus College in St. Peter, who had been the Republican Party's sacrificial-lamb candidate against Hubert Humphrey for US Senate in 1976. Brekke won just 39 percent of the vote in that Senate race. He was an earnest man who had not held elective office before and thus lacked a genuine political base. That made him vulnerable to a primary challenge, which he got from a maverick in the Republican ranks, former Minneapolis mayor Charlie Stenvig. Brekke defeated Stenvig in the September 12 primary by thirty-six thousand votes. It was an uninspiring send-off into the general election.[11]

Brekke's campaign theme was a familiar one. He faulted my support for Election Day registration, arguing, as Arlen Erdahl had four years earlier, that Election Day registration was subject to fraud. He told the *St. Cloud Times* that while I had been "persistent about getting people to the polls," I had "not been as eager to protect the validity and integrity" of election results. He said Election Day registration causes a "high rate of error," and that "voter confidence in the system will continue to erode" as a result.[12]

Notably, he provided no evidence that Election Day registration resulted in errors or a lack of "validity and integrity," because there was none. The law we passed in 1973 guards against that. In order to register to vote on Election Day, a voter needed to swear an oath about the accuracy of his or her address and present a valid driver's license or government-issued ID card. If a would-be voter lacked those things, another registered voter in the precinct could sign an oath vouching that he or she knew that the registrant lived in the precinct. (In 1985, we began allowing college student IDs to suffice for Election Day registration; in the 1990s, we added a recent utility bill or rent or bank statement bearing a voter's current name and address as sufficient proof of residency.) Any new registrant caught voting more than once in the same election is guilty of a felony under Minnesota law, punishable by at least a year in prison. That stiff penalty is intended to deter fraud, and it works. It's almost unheard of in Minnesota for a voter to cast more than one ballot in the same election. A study produced in 2012 by the Carnegie-Knight News21 program found there were a total of ten cases of fraud and no cases of voter impersonation reported in Minnesota between 2000 and 2012.[13]

Election Day registration was available in 1978 for the third state election in a row. It had been used by nearly 935,000 Minnesotans in the primary and general elections in 1974 and 1976. That's more than half of the number of voters that my office expected to turn out in the 1978 midterm election in the state. I knew I was on solid ground when I said that Minnesotans understood and liked same-day registration, and wanted it to stay on the books. As the *Minneapolis Tribune* said as it endorsed me for a second term, Gerald Brekke's arguments were "unconvincing."[14]

Independent-Republicans did so well in 1978 that pundits dubbed the year the Minnesota Massacre. The IR Party won both US Senate seats, the governorship, and the state auditor's office. But I won re-election with 52 percent of the vote, compared to Brekke's 44 percent and 4 percent for a third-party candidate. Attorney General Warren Spannaus, State Treasurer Jim Lord, and I were the only DFLers to win statewide that year. The House went from a 104–30 DFL majority at the start of the 1977 session to an almost unworkable 67–67 tie.[15]

A wave election like that one puts surviving, losing-party politicians in a new and often more favorable light. Almost immediately, my name was mentioned as someone with potential for higher office. A *Minneapolis Tribune* story two days after the election quoted Jeri Rasmussen, a leader of a group that had been cool to me, the DFL Feminist Caucus, listing people to whom she and her allies would henceforward look as candidates for top offices. On Jeri's list were Spannaus, then–St. Paul mayor George Latimer, and me.[16]

• • •

The thought of running for governor or US senator one day had occurred to me too, as I imagine it does to most state-level politicians. It often starts as a passing fancy. Now, for me, it was becoming an increasingly plausible option. A number of somewhat serendipitous events in the late 1970s thrust me into the limelight and gave me a chance to make a larger impression on the state's electorate.

For example, in 1977—as the state's highest-ranking female elected officeholder—I agreed to serve as the chair of the Minnesota Women's Meeting. It was an assembly of some four thousand women in St. Cloud on June 2–5, funded by Congress and organized under the direction of the National Commission on the Observance of International Women's Year, a United Nations–initiated series of events. Every state was authorized to conduct a similar meeting. The three-day gathering at St. Cloud State University was open to all comers—both women who considered themselves feminists and those who were skeptical of the changes feminists sought. On the agenda were scores of workshops on topics of interest to women. In its plenary sessions, the meeting was also tasked with adopting policy resolutions and electing delegates to be sent to the National Women's Conference in Houston, Texas, in November 1977.

I was at the podium during that meeting when two memorable things happened. The first was the opportunity Governor Rudy Perpich gave me to announce his appointment that day of Minnesota's first-ever female associate justice of the Minnesota Supreme Court, Rosalie Wahl. Perpich made the appointment late on June 3, a Friday afternoon, while he was in Hibbing, Minnesota, his hometown, preparing to be the featured speaker at his son's high school commencement ceremony that evening. Perpich well understood the historic significance of his decision and the joy it would produce at the women's meeting. He wanted the news to be announced in that setting, but he also wanted to keep his commitment to his son. His decision to allow me to break the story in that packed arena, with TV cameras rolling, was a gracious one that subtly signaled a close working relationship between the governor and me. The announcement brought a welcome moment of unity and elation to an event that was otherwise fraught with division.[17]

Another memorable development involved the divisions—primarily over abortion, but also over gay rights and the Equal Rights Amendment—that went on full display the next evening. I was again at the podium, presiding over the meeting's plenary session. I came to the convention in the company of a personal security guard, hired by the state because threats had been made against me. On the agenda were debate and action on thirty-two resolutions to be sent from Minnesota to the national meeting in Houston. The most controversial of the proposed resolutions was one calling for an end to "interference, open or subtle, with a woman's right to control her reproduction." Many participants arrived expecting a long night of intense discussion. But the politically savvy members of a steering committee that had prepared the draft resolutions had a different plan. They were veterans of political conventions, schooled in parliamentary procedure. They knew they had the votes because the meeting had attracted a lopsidedly feminist crowd. Early in Saturday night's proceedings, Koryne Horbal rose to call the question on the entire batch of resolutions. That nondebatable motion passed, and so did the entire slate of resolutions. As a majority of those present cheered, some 250 anti-abortion participants walked out in protest.[18]

My name as chair would be on the letter forwarding those resolutions to the national meeting in Houston. That meant my name would also be on a lawsuit—which was ultimately tossed out of court—objecting to the validity of some of the meeting's actions. What's more, my name would be linked with the meeting for good and for ill as Minnesotans debated its significance and consequences. The Morrison County DFL executive committee voted 24–0 in late June to call for my resignation as secretary of state, which prompted the Winona County DFL executive committee a few weeks later to pass a resolution of praise and support for me. The Winona County resolution said I had shown "dedication to advance the status of Minnesota women through the promotion of discussion of women's issues." My name had become linked in Minnesota politics with women's rights as well as voting rights.[19]

Unsolicited attention came my way again when the Minnesota House convened on January 3, 1979. A 67–67 tie in the House's partisan caucuses was unprecedented in Minnesota history, and exceedingly rare in other states. But this much was certain: until a Speaker could be elected, the House's presiding officer was the secretary of state. Blessedly, that circumstance lasted just five days. A deal was reached that led to Independent-Republican representative Rod Searle's election as Speaker on January 8. Stories were written and broadcast before the session's start about the pivotal role I would play and speculating that my career could rise or fall based on how I wielded the House's gavel. But the forecasted drama did not materialize. I did my constitutional duty without incident (and with considerable help from the House's esteemed chief clerk, Edward Burdick, and legal advice from attorney and DFL state representative Ray Faricy of St. Paul).[20]

More drama came to the Minnesota House five months later. Representative Robert Pavlak, a St. Paul police officer and a Republican from West St. Paul who had won his fifth term by just 321 votes, was found guilty of violating state campaign laws in 1978. Four days before the election, he had distributed an editorial endorsing him published by the *St. Paul Pioneer Press* that contained two errors about the record of his opponent, DFL state representative Arnold Kempe. The

Convening the Minnesota House of Representatives in 1979. I was the presiding officer for five days, while the parties worked out an agreement to handle the tie in House seats.

Minnesota Supreme Court said that Pavlak was aware of the errors and thus was responsible for distributing falsehoods in violation of the state's campaign practices laws. On a bitterly disputed 67–66 party-line vote—with Pavlak not voting—the House removed him from office. Pavlak announced immediately that he would run for the seat in a June 19 special election to fill the vacancy his ouster had caused.

That's where I came into the story. On the advice of Attorney General Warren Spannaus, I directed my staff to disallow Pavlak to file as a candidate for the special election. My new office director, Tom Durand, broke that news to Pavlak when he showed up at our elections counter intending to file for the seat. It wasn't a comfortable encounter—made less so, Tom recalls, by the fact that Pavlak was dressed in his police uniform and wore his pistol at the time. Spannaus cited a state law that barred a legislator from seeking election to the same seat from which he had been removed during the same term as the removal. The law was pretty clear, we thought. But Republicans and some in the media accused Warren and me of engineering a DFL plot to block the Independent-Republican candidate best able to hold the seat for the GOP—and thereby break the 67–67 tie and shift control of the House back to the DFL in the 1980 session. That charge lingered in the air when on May 25, a week after Pavlak's ouster, the Minnesota Supreme Court unanimously ruled that Pavlak could file for the seat. The justices found that the law Spannaus had cited was unconstitutional. That unexpected outcome left Warren and me looking like party hacks, simply for doing our jobs.[21]

• • •

With heightened partisanship becoming the new normal in state government, Tom Durand and I resolved to focus on our core businesses: election and corporate law administration. After years of legislative neglect and episodic amendment, the laws governing both of our functions were overdue for cleanup. Election laws in particular had become riddled with inconsistencies. Tom had been supervisor of elections in Anoka County prior to coming to work for me, and was well aware of the problems the messy election statutes were causing at the local level.

At his urging, I appointed a task force to present to the legislature a draft recodification of those statutes—that is, to rewrite them for greater clarity, logic, and simplicity but not to alter their substance. If the task force believed changes in substance were needed, they could make recommendations to the legislature, but could not include those ideas in their draft. Tom agreed to staff the task force, which was comprised of several county auditors, city clerks, a representative of the League of Women Voters, and legislators from both parties and chambers. We were fortunate that Anoka County attorney Robert W. Johnson, who had first been elected to that post in 1950, agreed to be the task force's chair. He was not only among the most respected county attorneys in the state but also an authority on election law. He led a hard-working group that understood the importance of its assignment. The initial phase of the task force's work was ready for legislative action in 1981; other components went to the legislature in subsequent years. That gave me a lot of explaining to do on my annual post-session tours to meet with local officials.[22]

We also continued to promote voting in general and Election Day registration. The 1980 election gave us much to talk about. More than two million ballots were cast on November 4 that year, 433,000 of them by people registering to vote on Election Day. The number of votes set a new Minnesota record, and the state's turnout led the nation again. But as a percentage of the eligible population, turnout was just under 72 percent, the lowest in Minnesota in a presidential election in thirty years. Minnesotans evidently were not enamored with the choice between the winner, Republican Ronald Reagan, or the loser, President Jimmy Carter, despite Vice President Walter Mondale's Minnesota roots. Carter and Mondale carried the state by eighty-one thousand votes. Third-party candidate John Anderson had one of his strongest showings in the nation in Minnesota, garnering 8.4 percent of the vote.

I wasn't surprised by those results. By mid-1979, I had concluded that President Carter was not politically healthy enough to win a second term. Galloping inflation, sporadic shortages of oil and gasoline, and the revolution in Iran, with the taking of American diplomats as hostages, led to a widespread sense that Carter was not succeeding as president. I feared that his unpopularity would drive down turnout, potentially costing Democrats control of the US House and Senate. I had long admired Massachusetts senator Edward Kennedy. When he signaled a willingness to replace Carter as the Democratic presidential candidate, I decided to publicly support him. Along with US representative Rick Nolan, I cochaired the Kennedy campaign in Minnesota in 1980. It was a long-shot mission in Walter Mondale's home state, and ultimately unsuccessful. And though I emphasized that I had no beef with Mondale—I often said "It's the vice president's job to support the president"—Mondale's friends in the DFL Party now had reason to have a beef with me.[23]

I opted to be a candidate for a third term as secretary of state in 1982. But everywhere I went in 1981 and early 1982, people asked me, "What are you going to do next, Joan?" The next step that many of them had in mind for me was a bid for lieutenant governor on the 1982 DFL ticket. There were two other possibilities for a DFL climber that year—governor and US senator. But Warren Spannaus, the former DFL Party state chairman who had been attorney general for a dozen years, was seen as a prohibitive favorite for the DFL endorsement for governor. And the senator who was up for reelection in 1982, moderate Republican Dave Durenberger, looked tough to beat. I decided to stay visible, stay available, and see what opportunities might come.

To my surprise, the opportunity that arose was one I could not accept. Former DFL Governor Rudy Perpich, defeated by Governor Al Quie in 1978, returned to Minnesota in April 1982 after several years of working in Vienna, Austria, for Minnesota's Control Data Corporation. Quie had opted to not seek a second term after a distressing run of state budget deficits. The open gubernatorial seat lured Perpich back into politics. He wanted his old job back. His plan to win it involved letting Spannaus have his day at the DFL state convention, then beating him for the nomination in the September primary. I had heard through the party grapevine that Rudy wanted to choose a woman as his running mate. Before 1982, no woman had been a major-party candidate for lieutenant governor, let alone served in that post.

Rudy and his wife, Lola, took me out to breakfast not long before the DFL convention. Their pitch was direct: I was his first choice as a running mate, Rudy announced. If I wanted the position, it was mine. He outlined in general terms the role he saw for me in the coming campaign and in his second administration, should he win. It was flattering and tempting. But I declined. I believed that running with Perpich would burn the bridges with the DFL establishment that I had already strained by backing Kennedy over Carter and Mondale in 1980. If we won, it might be awkward for me to quickly turn around and run for higher office in 1984. If we lost—and in my judgment, chances were fairly high that we would—my political career would come to a screeching halt. I would be out of office and out of a job.

I believed there was a chance that Spannaus would call with the same offer. I quietly decided to also decline if he did. But on May 25, Warren made a more conventional choice. His running mate would be state representative Carl Johnson of St. Peter, a genial fellow with a Swedish accent whose legislative specialty was K–12 education. Johnson provided the urban-rural geographic balance that was the time-honored formula for building a Minnesota political ticket, but that failed to acknowledge gender or racial diversity. A howl went up from feminists. "Spannaus Choice Upsets Women," said the headline in the St. Cloud newspaper. The Associated Press asked Rudy Perpich for his reaction to Spannaus's choice. Perpich said, "He should have chosen Joan Growe."[24]

I was asked whether I would offer my name to the convention as a candidate for lieutenant governor anyway, regardless of Spannaus's wishes. I said no. I knew Warren well enough to know that running with him would likely be a difficult experience, for me or any other woman. A native of St. Paul's hardscrabble East Side, Spannaus was a conventional thinker about social matters and was highly averse to controversy or scandal. He wasn't comfortable breaking any barriers. As DFL state chairman in the late 1960s, he went so far as to refuse to travel to party events with party chairwoman Koryne Horbal, not because of any animus toward her but because he feared that gossip about their relationship might ensue.[25]

I went to the June 4–5 convention in Duluth to seek and receive the endorsement for a third term as secretary of state. I then sat in the balcony at the Duluth Entertainment and Convention Center

(DECC) and watched the convention endorse Carl Johnson for lieutenant governor over state representative Arlene Lehto of Duluth. Arlene had been so angry over Spannaus's choice that she launched a futile, eleventh-hour challenge to Johnson. As I watched, I might have spent a few moments questioning whether I had misjudged the gubernatorial contest that year. Maybe Spannaus was not as strong a candidate as I'd thought. Maybe Perpich's willingness to make bold moves and his determination to break barriers for women—which would be in greater evidence a few days later, when he named St. Paul business owner and feminist leader Marlene Johnson as his running mate—would give him an edge in the primary and general elections that year.

But most of my thoughts in the DECC balcony were running well ahead of the developments on the convention floor below. I decided it was time for me to make a plan for 1984. I wanted to be a senator.

7

Running "As a Woman"

A trip I made in July 1983 to Washington, DC, caught the attention of Washington-based *Minneapolis Star and Tribune* reporter Steve Berg. I was making the DC rounds that any serious would-be Democratic candidate for the US Senate would make, calling on leaders of labor, civil rights, and environmental groups; introducing myself to journalists; recruiting potential staffers, pollsters, and consultants; and raising money. Berg noticed one distinctive thing about my late-afternoon fundraising gathering: its attendees were primarily women.[1]

"Growe is trying to take advantage of what may be her top political asset: her gender," Berg reported. "There is a special commitment among Democratic women to elect at least one woman to the US Senate next year." It galled the feminists in the Democratic Party that only two women served in the US Senate that year, both of them Republicans.[2]

The notion was far from new that women make different political choices than men, and that their choices deserve to be reflected in election outcomes. That idea helped propel the long crusade for women's suffrage. But not until a full sixty years after American women got the right to vote did pollsters and pundits see a widening difference—a gender gap—in men's and women's preferences in presidential politics. The winner of the 1980 election, Republican Ronald Reagan, won 55 percent of the votes cast by men but 47 percent of those cast by women. That was deemed a meaningful difference. The 1980 election set a pattern that persists today: women remain more inclined than men to support the Democratic Party's candidates.[3]

I set out to turn that difference to my advantage. My candidacy became official on October 2, 1983, at a well-orchestrated event at Leo and Marion Fogarty's farm in Le Sueur County near Belle Plaine that emphasized my rural roots. But all that year, I had been making plans and taking initial steps toward a bid for the US Senate against Minnesota's one-term Republican senator, Rudy Boschwitz. I had become convinced in 1982 that I was ready to run for one of the two brass rings (governor and senator) in state politics, and that Minnesotans were ready to elect a woman—specifically me.[4]

My 1982 election to a third term as secretary of state encouraged my thinking. I led the DFL ticket with 59.36 percent of the vote, defeating a little-known Republican, Mark Hanson, a twenty-five-year-old political neophyte who campaigned on the wrongheaded idea that the secretary of state should be appointed by the governor, not elected. Admittedly, my winning percentage was just a fraction higher than that won by the DFL candidate for attorney general with the politically enviable name Hubert H. "Skip" Humphrey III. He scored 59.18 percent. And my victory did not produce the political wallop that came with Rudy Perpich's solid win over Republican businessman Wheelock Whitney. Perpich's election signaled Minnesotans' willingness to embrace new ideas for the sake of achieving a strong position in the emerging global economy. As I began to sense at the 1982 DFL convention, conventional Warren Spannaus wasn't a match for a colorful former governor with compelling ideas about how state government could be employed to jump-start Minnesota's economy. Perpich defeated Spannaus in the September 14 primary by nearly twenty-eight thousand votes, and went on to win 58.76 percent of the vote in November.

The DFL's overall showing that year also left me feeling good about a Senate bid. The party won strong majorities in both the House and Senate, and kept control of the state treasurer's office despite a divisive primary for that nomination. However, the picture wasn't entirely rosy. DFLers missed the mark in the 1982 Senate race, in which Republican senator Dave Durenberger won a second term. His opponent, DFL candidate Mark Dayton, was a youthful state-agency head in Perpich's first term. He had no problem with name recognition, as the scion of a retailing family whose name is synonymous in Minnesota with the state's finest department stores. But Dayton had not previously held elective office, and, at age thirty-five and running a largely self-financed campaign, he was seen as an unseasoned politician spending his own money to run. That was a far cry from the image I would bring to a Senate race.

My opponent would be quite different too. While Durenberger was part of the Minnesota Independent-Republican Party's Young Turk moderate wing, Boschwitz was a Reagan conservative. Durenberger's faction had been dominant in the state in the 1960s, but was losing its grip on the party and the electorate by the 1980s. Whereas Durenberger was at work in the Senate on the policy complexities of revenue sharing, education, health care, and environmental protection, Boschwitz exhibited more interest in politics than policy. A fifty-two-year-old German immigrant and the millionaire owner of the Plywood Minnesota home improvement retail chain, Boschwitz was an indefatigable fundraiser for Republican candidates. As the state's first Jewish senator, his interest in America's support of Israel was clear. In many ways, he was an old-style Republican cold warrior—an anticommunist, pro-military hawk on foreign policy. I was not, and I did not think a majority of Minnesotans were, either.[5]

What's more, Boschwitz had won his seat in 1978 because of an unforced DFL error: Governor Wendell Anderson's self-appointment to the US Senate. Replace Anderson on the DFL ballot with a more appealing name, and Boschwitz could lose. Put atop the same ballot a Minnesotan's name—that of former vice president Walter Mondale, a top contender for the Democratic presidential nomination—and 1984 could be a very good year for this DFLer to run.

Or so I reasoned.

Still, those facts did not blind me to a less encouraging reality. Minnesota still had a meager record of electing women. The 1983 legislature convened with twenty-eight women members—a new record, but still just 14 percent of the total 201 seats. In 1983 Minnesota had two female associate justices on the Minnesota Supreme Court. That was more than any other state at the time, but still just two-sevenths of the total. Four of eighty-seven Minnesota county attorneys (the state's elected prosecutors) were women, as were six percent of county commissioners and five percent of the state's mayors. For the first time in state history, two women held state constitutional offices, with Lieutenant Governor Marlene Johnson joining me in that club of six. But a *Minneapolis Star and Tribune* story highlighting Johnson's new status also reported that after eight years in the office, I still received letters addressed to "Mr. Secretary."[6]

Clearly, women had made progress in Minnesota politics. It had become plausible to claim that my gender could be an asset in a Senate race. But as I would discover, running "as a woman" in 1984 for a top political prize would bring challenges too. (I was often asked what it was like to run for office "as a woman." I wish I had thought to respond the way US representative Patricia Schroeder of Colorado did when she ran for president four years later: "I didn't realize I had any other option.")

I let it be known shortly after the 1982 election that I was serious about pursuing a Senate bid, advising the state's reporters that mentioning my name among likely candidates would be appropriate. I then made one of my best personnel decisions. Elaine Voss of Blaine, the state DFL Party's executive secretary and a former Anoka County elections director, agreed to become my deputy in March 1983. Elaine's professional background included stints as a nurse and an instructor of nursing. Her personal story included marriage to Gordon Voss, a professor of mechanical engineering who tried his hand at politics at Elaine's urging and wound up serving sixteen years in the Minnesota House. Elaine was my near-contemporary in age. She was whip-smart, politically savvy, witty, and a source of calm amid chaos. She was just the manager I needed in charge at the State Office Building while I stumped the state—and just the advisor with whom I wanted to strategize when I returned.

From the outset, I laid plans for a three-phase Senate campaign—first the party endorsement, then the DFL primary, and finally the general election. Candidates with means and/or big names sometimes skip step one (as, for example, Mark Dayton did in 2010 when he ran successfully for governor). I had no intention of doing so. I lacked the deep pockets of a Dayton or the universal name recognition of a Perpich. But the main reason I opted to pursue party endorsement was that it represented the people-to-people politics that had been a hallmark of every Growe campaign to date. I knew that a US Senate campaign could not be run like the door-to-door women's brigade of 1972 in Minnetonka and Eden Prairie. It would involve mass-media messaging, polling, consultants, and money, money, money. But I wanted it to start with a core group of several thousand people who knew me personally and who would give up a number of springtime nights and weekends in order to advance my candidacy at party conventions. Those would be the people who would talk up my candidacy to their friends and family, volunteer their time in the fall to deliver my literature, write checks that would keep my ads on the air and my plane in the sky, and see to it that I was met with friendly faces wherever my campaign plane landed. Those people were the real advantage that the DFL endorsement would bring, and I didn't want to run without them.

I knew I would not be a shoo-in for party endorsement. The men in the party who thought it was their turn to try for the Senate were not about to step aside for me. I considered a primary challenge

Announcing my candidacy for Minnesota senator on the farm of Leo and Marian Fogarty in Derrynane Township, Le Sueur County, October 2, 1983

after the state convention a strong possibility. And if I crossed those two hurdles, the battle against Boschwitz, who was both personally wealthy and a prodigious fundraiser, would be the toughest of all.

I assembled a campaign staff with those three contests in mind. Andrea Christianson, who had managed a successful Hennepin County commissioner's race in 1982, agreed to see me through the convention as campaign manager; I later recruited state senator Steve Novak of New Brighton to manage the campaign in the fall. One who would be at my side through each phase was Bob Meek, a former DFL Party staffer, Hubert Humphrey speechwriter, and Carter-Mondale state campaign director who came on early in 1983 as a media consultant and spokesperson. Bob is a very able guy with a big heart and dedication to the work of building a more inclusive society.

I was thrilled when Vance Opperman agreed to be my treasurer. A prominent attorney and son of a well-known businessman, Opperman was a respected figure within the DFL Party, because of both his fundraising and his work at every level of the party. He brought instant credibility to my campaign. Vance brought with him the talents of Ted Grindal, a young attorney in his firm who had served me well as a legislative intern eleven years earlier and a faithful campaign driver in 1974. I also hired a staff fundraising team led by Carole Faricy that included Ham Thompson, future Minneapolis city council member Scott Benson, and volunteer coordinator Pat Lind. All but Carole pitched in as part of my state convention team as well.

• • •

The quest for state-convention delegate support is often done quietly, below the media's radar. It involves wooing and winning over longtime local party activists whose support often brings with it the backing of a group of delegates from an entire county or region. I was frequently on the road or on the phone with such people in 1983. As the political season progressed, I enlisted organizing help from several energetic young DFL activists: Bob Seng, Gary Cohen, and future DFL state chair Rick Stafford. Still later in the process, my daughter, Colleen, who lives in New York, came home on weekends to function as my surrogate at DFL meetings I could not attend. A petite person, she carried with her a small homemade podium to make her more visible to people on stage. It had been built by Tom Durand, the office manager in the secretary of state's office. That homemade box became a talking point and a campaign emblem of sorts for her.

I was also in Washington in 1983, not just in July but several times, seeking attention. Any media mentions of my candidacy were sent straight to the Democratic Senate Campaign Committee (DSCC) in Washington. I wanted that committee's notice. It has a great deal to say about the flow of national money and talent into US Senate races around the country. We knew that two of my likely rivals, US representative James Oberstar of Minnesota's Eighth District and former senator Wendell Anderson, had plenty of Washington ties. We wanted to make sure people at the DSCC and its allied groups knew that Oberstar and Anderson weren't the only strong candidates in Minnesota. Our plea: Don't line up too soon with a candidate. Wait until after the state convention. Fortunately, I made a fast friend of a woman on the DSCC staff, Audrey Sheppard, who became my Washington watchdog and advocate. She saw to it that national resources did not flow to anyone in Minnesota too soon.

I was particularly grateful for Audrey's help because I wasn't the only woman on the DSCC's radar that year. By the time all the nomination contests were settled, women would be the Democratic nominees in six states. The Republican Party wasn't far behind. It had female Senate nominees in four states, including Kansas, where Nancy Landon Kassebaum was seeking a second term. She and Paula Hawkins of Florida were the Senate's two women members. But a number of the other Democratic female challengers could fairly be called token candidates making long-shot bids in GOP-dominated states. Minnesota, on the other hand, was a true swing state in Senate politics and a state with a long Democratic "blue" streak in presidential elections. I could be seen in Washington as someone with a real chance to win.

By year's end, the DFL endorsement field was set. My chief rivals, as expected, were Oberstar and Anderson. Also running was Hennepin County commissioner John Derus. Other DFL luminaries who had been mentioned in the early going, including Mark Dayton, Warren Spannaus, Skip Humphrey, state Senate leader Roger Moe, and state House Speaker Harry Sieben Jr., opted not to run. Perhaps they perceived more clearly than I did that an economic rebound had begun that would work to the advantage of the Republican president and his allies, even in Walter Mondale's home state.

Our crucial first challenge was to get our supporters elected as future convention delegates at the DFL precinct caucuses on March 20. Without a straw poll or statewide reporting mechanism then, it wasn't easy to claim with certainty that we "won" the caucuses. But the informal reporting network we'd established convinced Andrea Christianson and me that we had out-organized and out-performed the others, and would likely go into the state DFL convention in the lead.

Convincing others that we were running ahead of the pack was another matter. An assessment of my political potency published by the *Minneapolis Star and Tribune* in June 1983 had remarkable staying power. "Growe has her political roots in the DFL's liberal and feminist wings," it said, implying that I might be more liberal than the party's mainstream. The analysis then acknowledged that I had "built successful alliances throughout the party" with three statewide campaigns. But it added a kicker that wouldn't die: "Party insiders are watching to see whether she has also acquired the fundraising and organizational skills required for a Senate race."[7]

The fact that I'd been exhibiting those skills with better results than any other candidate went unacknowledged, then and for many months thereafter. It didn't seem to matter that I had raised the most money prior to the DFL state convention (Oberstar was consistently in second place) or that polls of delegates before the convention showed me in the lead. Reporters kept asking the same tiring questions. "Can you raise enough money to wage an effective campaign? Do you have the kind of organization that can win statewide?" It felt as if I had to be twice as good, twice as assertive, and twice as nice as the other candidates just to be seen as keeping pace.[8]

The question that particularly annoyed me was, "Are you sure you're tough enough to be a US senator?" I'd reply with a laugh, "Explain to me what you mean by strong. If you mean, can I lift as much weight as John Derus, probably not." (Derus is a burly fellow, well over six feet tall. I'm about five feet five.)

When retorts like that didn't quash the toughness question, I decided it was time to tell Minnesotans more about myself. I remembered what I had learned in the secretary of state's office about the advisability in public life of telling one's own story rather than waiting for someone else to do it. In late May 1983, I called Lori Sturdevant of the *Minneapolis Star and Tribune* and offered her a long interview about my personal life, including my stint as a recipient of Aid to Families with Dependent Children in the summer of 1964. Sturdevant's story was splashed atop the front page of the paper on June 3—a Sunday, the newspaper's biggest circulation day. She quoted me at length:

> Now, 20 years later, I can say I wish it had not happened, and I wish my life had been different, but I have a lot more compassion for alcoholism, for families who have a history of abuse, and for people who have to depend on government for assistance. It left me with a sense that most people do not want to take assistance, but you never know when you're going to need it. And if you treat people with a certain amount of dignity at the time, I think you're going to get it returned in many ways. I think that has shaped a great deal of how I feel about government and about issues. . . .
>
> If people know what I have lived through in my life, they know a political campaign is nothing I can't handle. I've been through things that have tested my strength more than that.[9]

The response to the story was overwhelmingly positive. But questions and comments that alluded to my strength persisted throughout my 1984 campaign. So did questions probing my family life. "Who is taking care of your kids while you're out campaigning?" I would be asked. From a practical perspective, the question was unwarranted. My three eldest children were grown and out of the house, and Patrick was a senior in high school by then. As always, I tried to answer with a smile. But I knew what was behind those questions. They were really asking, "Can a woman be a US senator?"

• • •

State convention delegates arrived on Saturday, June 16, at the St. Paul Civic Center knowing that they were in for a long day and night. I arrived wearing an easy-to-spot bright red suit and comfortable flat shoes, dressed for the political equivalent of hand-to-hand combat. I was accompanied by my three elder children, Michael, Colleen, and David, who were ready to sell delegates on their mom. To my campaign's dismay, the convention's rules committee had failed to adopt the customary "drop-off" rule that would compel trailing candidates to leave the race at some point in the balloting. That omission guaranteed that the convention was in for a four-way battle for many hours to come.

Our floor operation was old-school—no walkie-talkies or computer modeling. Ham Thompson of my campaign staff, who coordinated my squadron of delegate trackers on the floor, didn't trust the then-emerging convention technology. We used triplicate paper forms and human runners to deliver news about each ballot's totals from the tabulation room to the floor. As a result, my staffer Scott Benson remembers, we were consistently able to deliver results to our county coordinators faster than the other campaigns, giving us precious extra minutes for one-on-one persuasion on the floor. Our system served us well. I led on the first ballot and every ballot thereafter. Oberstar was consistently in second place, followed by Derus, then Anderson. Anderson's support waned and both Oberstar's and mine grew a bit as the balloting progressed through the afternoon and evening. But Anderson, a proud former governor, refused to acknowledge that he was beaten and drop out. Though his support dwindled below 100 of the 1,220 delegates at the convention, those supporters included some of the party's leading lights. AFL-CIO president Dave Roe kept a core of top labor leaders in Anderson's camp. US representative Martin Sabo, the Speaker of the state House during my tenure in that body, was purportedly neutral, but I suspected that he too was backing Anderson and counseling him not to yield. After six ballots, each one taking nearly two hours to tally, Anderson went to the podium to release his delegates. But he did not drop out of the race. He made clear that if the convention deadlocked, he was still available.

Derus, making his first try for statewide office, followed Anderson's lead after the eighth ballot.

Tensions had been running high between Oberstar and me. The public face of our disagreement was the abortion issue. Oberstar was among the most ardent Democratic opponents of legal abortion in the US House. He was often invited as the keynote speaker at gatherings of anti-abortion groups in Minnesota and around the country. He called a news conference the weekend before the convention to attack me for "going off the deep end" in support of women's right to the reproductive care of their choice. But something else he said at that press conference revealed more of his hostility to my candidacy. He charged that I "lacked substance" on other issues, and that I was emphasizing abortion rights because I was uncomfortable with other issues.[10]

That was nonsense. Abortion had not been a major theme of my campaign. I'd been talking primarily about the economic and war-and-peace issues that united Democrats and separated them from Rudy Boschwitz. Like Oberstar, I wanted to rein in military spending and impose a freeze on nuclear weapons development. Like Oberstar, I wanted an end to military aid to repressive governments in Central America. (To that end, I took a ten-day fact-finding trip to that region in late 1983 so that I could speak more knowledgably about the situation there.) Like Oberstar, I wanted to scale back the 1981 Reagan tax cuts to curb rising federal deficits, though I was somewhat more willing to raise taxes on the wealthy to finance more federal investment in education and health care. I told reporters after Oberstar's press conference that his were the "hysterical comments of a losing campaign."[11]

I didn't say aloud what I was really thinking: they were the comments of a man who did not like the admission of a woman to his club. He was a former congressional chief of staff and a ten-year member of Congress who thought he was at the head of the line to be the state's US senator. I was getting in his way. I wasn't part of the old-boys' network of DFL men who often met at the clubby Lexington restaurant in St. Paul for private fundraisers for their friends. Those fellows didn't hate me personally. If pressed, they probably would have said they rather liked me—but then hasten to add that they did not think I could win a Senate election. They wouldn't own up to the bias behind that view.

At 5:30 AM Sunday—after fourteen ballots—the four candidates were summoned to a private huddle with DFL Party chair Mary Monahan. Monahan was new to that role and was the first woman to hold the post. She was also strongly anti-abortion, though officially neutral in the Senate endorsement fight. She allowed each of us to be accompanied by one staffer. I brought with me my young convention floor leader, Ted Grindal. We found ourselves confronted with not one staffer per candidate but multiple party leaders supporting Oberstar and Anderson. At most endorsing conventions, party leaders push delegates to rally behind the candidate who leads the balloting, as I had on every ballot. That was not Monahan's intent. Instead, it became clear that the purpose of Monahan's meeting was to convince me to drop out. She would then adjourn the convention with no endorsement. We would take our fight for the nomination into the September 11 primary. It was a case of the big boys ganging up on me, with Monahan's help. I learned from a reporter after the convention that the other three candidates' leaders had been secretly meeting in the back of the convention hall all day and evening.

I thought dropping out would be a terrible thing to do to my delegates, who had stayed with me through a sleepless night and deserved a victory. Our huddle ended without a resolution. But when the next two ballots continued the stalemate, Monahan reconvened the candidates and pressed for an agreement to bring the battle to an end. Reluctantly, I agreed to one more ballot—number seventeen. If I did not pass the 60-percent finish line, all of us would bow out.

I held my breath when the tally was announced. I was 2.74 percentage points shy of the 60-percent mark. Crestfallen, I went to the podium and told the delegates that I had given my word, and I keep my word. I announced that I would end my quest for endorsement and carry my campaign to the primary.

I expected the deflated convention to then move on to other business. But my delegates would have none of it. One of my supporters, Minneapolis attorney Mary Ellen Tisdale, came to the microphone with a motion to continue the balloting. The candidates may have

On the floor during the 1984 DFL convention, June 18, 1984. Marlin Levinson, Minneapolis Star and Tribune

made a deal, she said, but the delegates had not been party to it. Delegates, not candidates, control the convention, she argued. Her motion prevailed, to my team's surprise and delight. Two ballots later—on ballot nineteen—I passed the requisite 732-vote threshold with 22 votes to spare. My supporters then set up a chant—"We want Joan!"—until I reappeared in the arena.

Oberstar's camp immediately cried foul and claimed that the convention's action was not valid. Frankly, I was not sure it was, at first. But St. Paul mayor George Latimer convinced me otherwise. Endorsement is the convention's to bestow, he said, and I had won it. Then he went to the podium to introduce my acceptance remarks. "Some people are saying an endorsement that takes this long to get won't be worth anything," Latimer told the delegates as the clock approached noon on Sunday. "They're wrong. You're going to make it worth something," he said to loud cheers. I hoped he was right.[12]

• • •

The endorsement proved its worth in subsequent days, to this extent: It helped convince first Derus, then Oberstar, then Anderson to end their Senate bids. It also brought other DFL officials and the state party's biggest name, former vice president Walter Mondale, in line behind my candidacy. The teachers' union and the state AFL-CIO gave me their official blessing. Massachusetts senator Edward Kennedy, whose presidential campaign I had backed in 1980, called me at home the day after the convention, offering his help. Kennedy was exceedingly loyal to those who stood by him.[13]

But endorsement did not clear the primary field for me. State Treasurer Robert Mattson Jr. had said for weeks that were I endorsed, he intended to challenge me. Given his political history and that of his namesake father, former state attorney general Robert Mattson Sr., I fully expected him to make good on his threat. The Mattsons were black sheep in the DFL family, and the son had been annoyingly successful in playing that role.

The father was an Iron Range native, a decorated World War II veteran, and an attorney. He succeeded Walter Mondale as attorney general when Mondale was appointed to Hubert Humphrey's US Senate seat after the 1964 election made Humphrey vice president. He did not run for the attorney general's seat in his own right in 1966. But even before Governor Rudy Perpich made good on his promise to put the first woman on the Minnesota Supreme Court in 1977, Mattson told Perpich that he intended to run against her, whoever she may be. His 1978 challenge to newly appointed Justice Rosalie Wahl ranks among the nastiest judicial elections in state history. He seriously distorted Wahl's record as he claimed that because she had written dissenting opinions in several criminal cases, she was soft on crime and disrespectful of state law. The state's judicial establishment rallied to Wahl's defense, assuring her a healthy margin of victory and ending the senior Mattson's political career.[14]

But the younger Mattson, who was thirteen years my junior, kept the family name in front of the state's voters with a series of bids for office, often challenging party-endorsed candidates in primary elections. That's what he did when he ran unsuccessfully for secretary of state in 1970, successfully for state auditor in 1974, and successfully for state treasurer in 1982. The party refused to endorse him (or anyone else) when he sought reelection in 1978. He lost that bid to future Independent-Republican governor Arne Carlson, even as his dad was losing to Wahl in the same election. But Mattson Jr.'s comeback in 1982 revived his political career and inspired him to play the spoiler again against me. He borrowed heavily from the primary-winning 1978 playbook of another DFL maverick, Robert Short. As Short did to then–US representative Don Fraser of Minneapolis, Mattson tried to cast me as an über-liberal, citified champion of legal abortion, gun control, and excessive environmental regulations.

But Mattson was no Bob Short (who was a shrewd millionaire owner of multiple businesses, including the Texas Rangers baseball team and the Leamington Hotel in Minneapolis). Mattson had tried his hand at entrepreneurship with a barbecue restaurant chain in Naples, Florida. That had kept him in Florida rather than in the state treasurer's office in St. Paul for months at a time in 1983—a fact that *Minneapolis Star and Tribune* reporter Betty Wilson brought to light to damaging effect.[15]

I couldn't afford to ignore Mattson. But the risk he posed to my candidacy was not so much that he would win but more that he would leave my campaign depleted and limping into the difficult race against Boschwitz in the general election. I needed a primary victory that was decisive, but not too expensive.

Enter Minnesota's Groweing. That was the name given to a female-designed and female-led support network that popped up in the heat of summer to boost my campaign. It didn't originate with my campaign and was not coordinated by it. Rather, it was a truly independent entity that sought to get out the pro-Growe vote the old-fashioned way, through people-to-people organizing. It was the brainchild of a group of ten active women—women who knew something about how to get things done with more people power than money. The ten were loosely acquainted with each other and shared a common interest in feminism and politics, but were not already part of an organized group. Their ability to come together quickly and effectively was a marvel and a model worth sharing.

The founding ten were Linda Holstein, a Minneapolis attorney;

The Democratic primary, as depicted by Pioneer Press *cartoonist Jerry Fearing, July 9, 1984*

Virginia Greenman, a former Republican and a health consultant; Ruby Hunt, a Ramsey County commissioner; Myrna Myrofsky, an IT entrepreneur; Martha Norton, a St. Paul DFL activist; Kathleen Kennedy Scott, an arts and charities volunteer; Emily Ann Staples, a former state senator and future Hennepin County commissioner; Mary Vogel-Heffernan, an administrator at the University of Minnesota School of Architecture; Jean West, a St. Paul entrepreneur; and Barbara Stuhler, associate dean of continuing education at the University of Minnesota. Stuhler told the Minnesota's Groweing story in a 1986 book, *No Regrets: Minnesota Women and the Joan Growe Senatorial Campaign.* As she tells it, Minnesota's Groweing sprang up in mid-July from a shared sense among some of my strongest female supporters that my campaign was relying too much on money and not enough on volunteers. In other words, they said, it was the sort of campaign a man would run, rather than one built to take advantage of the particular political gifts of women.[16]

The corrective action they proposed was a hastily built pyramid scheme. The ten of them would each recruit ten friends, who would be

*Minnesota's Groweing campaign button
No. 1, 1974*

asked to recruit ten friends each, and so on, until at least one hundred thousand Minnesotans had committed to voting for me in the September 11 primary. Each commitment was rewarded with the receipt of a numbered, green-and-white Minnesota's Groweing button, for which recipients were asked, but not required, to pay a dollar, which was believed to be enough to cover the cost of buttons and information kits. Each committed person was supplied with material about me and my candidacy, and a reporting sheet with which to communicate the names and contact information of those recruited. Each recruiter was also instructed to make a get-out-the-vote reminder call to their recruitees on the eve of the primary. That was it. The total budget for the primary election effort, which included a huge kick-off breakfast at the Prom Center in St. Paul, was a modest $25,000. It was simple, it was frugal, and it engaged a lot of people and encouraged them to vote. In other words, it was my kind of politics. I was proud to receive Minnesota's Groweing button No. 1.

Minnesota's Groweing acknowledged that it fell short of its goal of one hundred thousand committed supporters by Labor Day—though how far short was never known. Nevertheless, it was a significant effort that undoubtedly increased turnout in a primary election that otherwise was not generating the voter interest I had expected. The DFL Senate primary was the only genuine contest on either party's statewide primary ballot, and it was fizzling. Mattson's campaign had little money and little ability to rally even anti-abortion forces, who seemed to have decided to sit out the primary and support Boschwitz in the general election. That choice was in keeping with a shift occurring throughout the nation in the 1980s. Increasingly, voters for whom abortion was an overriding issue—even those who had been lifelong Democrats—identified themselves as Republicans. Many such voters opted to not bother with the DFL primary, or so it appeared from Mattson's dismal vote totals. He won just 61,489 votes, compared to my 238,190. Two years later, he lost the DFL primary while seeking a second term as state treasurer and left Minnesota politics for good.[17]

• • •

I wasn't much buoyed by my big victory over Mattson. It came in an election with meager turnout. Just 18 percent of voters went to the polls. What's more, the numbers that were uppermost in my mind in September were the ones in a mid-August Minnesota Poll, the long-established, statewide poll conducted by the *Minneapolis Star and Tribune.* They were dismal. I trailed Boschwitz by 21 percentage points, 56 percent to 35 percent.[18]

Almost as discouraging were the poll's findings in the presidential race. In his home state, Walter Mondale had a statistically inconclusive 2 percentage-point lead over President Ronald Reagan, 46 percent to 44 percent. Like nearly every other DFL candidate in the state, I was hoping for a Mondale showing strong enough to pull me along. The poll warned us that the former vice president might not have any coattails to ride.[19]

After a rocky first two years in office marked by the worst economic distress Minnesota had experienced since the Great Depression, Reagan was on the rebound by 1984. His approval rating in national polls bottomed out at 35 percent in January 1983, and had risen steadily since then. The economy had righted itself, and the bombing of a US Marine barracks in Beirut and Reagan's invasion of Grenada, both in October 1983, prompted many Americans to rally around the president. Reagan also wore well with Americans. His Hollywood history and good looks, sunny disposition, and unabashed patriotism made him a likeable figure, even among people who were discomfited by his policies. *Boston Globe* columnist Ellen Goodman drew a parallel between my race with Boschwitz and the presidential contest. She

noted that both featured a "nice-guy" Republican incumbent challenged by an earnest Democrat who insisted on talking about arcane
national policies at a time when Americans weren't too unhappy with
their government.[20]

But polls also showed that a majority of Minnesotans agreed with
me, not Boschwitz, on a raft of issues. Minnesotans were with me, not
him, on support for a nuclear-weapons freeze and the Equal Rights
Amendment. Like me, they did not want to see cuts in Social Security; Boschwitz refused to take a "no-cut" pledge. By a small margin,
Minnesotans wanted abortion kept legal, as did I, unlike Boschwitz.

I'd been stumping the state to talk about those differences for
more than a year. I was much aided by my postconvention campaign
manager, Steve Novak, a state senator from New Brighton, and my
energetic assistant and driver, Bob Seng, who kept me moving each
day. But until Labor Day—a week before the primary election—my
campaign lacked the resources to take my case against Boschwitz to
the airwaves. By then, he had already been on the air intermittently
since March, starting with a huge ad buy that featured Minnesotans
thanking him for his constituent services work or for uncontroversial
positions he took, such as the extension of GI Bill benefits to cover
chemical dependency treatment. Those "Thanks, Sen. Boschwitz"
ads were highly effective. They were made possible by the huge
fundraising advantage he enjoyed. As of the end of September, he
had raised $5.2 million, compared with my $1.2 million. I was on pace
to raise a total of $1.6 million from donors, more than any previous
DFL Senate candidate. Yet I was outspent nearly four to one.[21]

I knew my chances weren't good. But I had a few cards to play,
and was determined to play them hard and well. One was to make the
most of what some pundits were calling the Year of the Woman. That
was their attempt to claim that Walter Mondale's selection of US representative Geraldine Ferraro of New York as his running mate would
bring more women to the polls and be a boon to other female candidates on the ballot. I could not avoid running "as a woman." Why
not tie myself to the vice-presidential candidate who had become the
most prominent woman in US politics? My campaign reached out
to Ferraro soon after she teamed up with Mondale, and secured her

commitment to sign a fundraising letter and come to Minnesota for fundraising and a rally.

She was good as her word. On a sunny September afternoon, Ferraro and I walked together onto the Hennepin County Government Center plaza, greeted by a roar from an estimated seven thousand fans. It wasn't the biggest crowd of the campaign for Ferraro, but it could not have been topped in enthusiasm. Ferraro captured the crowd's sense that they were witnessing a political turning point when she said that her candidacy and mine represented "a battle for women throughout this country, not only for today and tomorrow, but on into the next century." As for me, I sounded some of my favorite themes: "The time to be concerned about our future is not later. It's now. The time for arms control is not later. It's now. The time to register people to vote is not later, it's now."[22]

The flurry of news coverage—and the $200,000 in proceeds—that the Ferraro event generated bolstered my campaign's visibility. So did a new line of attack that began with TV ads in late September. I had been faulting Boschwitz for some time for his votes that increased the federal deficit and military spending while eliminating minimum Social Security benefits. Those issues did not appear to be moving many voters. I decided to call out Boschwitz for his failure to make public his tax returns, as I had done for the previous five years. My ad noted that millionaires like him benefited royally from the 1981 tax cut for which he had voted, and suggested that that windfall might be his reason for insisting that his tax returns remain private. "When a millionaire doesn't pay his fair share, we make up the difference," the ads said.[23]

Those ads finally pushed the polls in the right direction. A mid-October Minnesota Poll put us within 7 percentage points of Boschwitz among likely voters. While that showing buoyed us, it also mobilized Minnesota's Republican establishment in Boschwitz's defense. Letters to the editor started appearing claiming that I was "slinging mud." Boschwitz himself briefly aired, then withdrew, a radio ad with a sexist undertone: "Maybe it's a question of experience in dealing with complex problems, or maybe it's just a matter of judgment," the ad said of me.[24]

Then Dave Durenberger, who had just won reelection to the Senate two years earlier with a 6 percentage-point margin of victory, went to bat for Boschwitz. With a talking-head TV commercial and full-page newspaper ads, Durenberger scolded, "Mrs. Growe, you've gone too far." The "Mrs." struck me and a lot of my supporters as patronizing and demeaning. In public speech, I was usually addressed as Secretary Growe, just as he was addressed as Senator Durenberger. So did the ad's holier-than-thou tone: "Perhaps worst of all, Mrs. Growe, you are attempting to dirty the reputation a very good man has built with a lifetime of public service." I considered that a stretch in describing a fifty-three-year-old who had spent just six years in elective office. I thought that big names in the Democratic Party—say, Walter Mondale—would counter the Durenberger ads with an explanation that a US Senate candidate's financial history ought to be a matter of public record. But no one did.[25]

The reaction that disappointed me most was that of the editorial board of the state's largest newspaper. In other states, candidates that had called out their opponents' failure to release tax returns had the backing of journalists, whose ability to do their jobs depends on transparency in government. The issue was being used to good effect that year in Illinois by Democrat Paul Simon, who went on to unseat Republican senator Charles Percy—like Boschwitz, a millionaire businessman. But the *Minneapolis Star and Tribune*'s editorial on October 18 defended Boschwitz's tax secrecy and urged him to "stand firm." It argued that requests for disclosure of a candidate's finances were "likely to be harassment or prying" based on a false assumption of "bad character or wrongdoing" on the part of elected officials. I saw my request as consistent with the public's right to know about the potential conflicts of interest of someone entrusted to set national policy—not least tax policy. I thought that the public would see it my way—as national polls say they do today with regard to the tax returns of President Donald Trump.[26]

Polls at the end of the campaign said otherwise. They showed that the Republican suggestion that I was a "mean" person who was campaigning outside the normal bounds of propriety was working. Rather than continuing to narrow, the gap between Boschwitz and me widened at the end of October.

I had fresh anecdotal evidence that my gender continued to be a two-edged sword in the campaign. My son David, who campaigned for me full time without salary after graduating with a business major from Gonzaga University in May 1984, came home from an on-air interview at a Willmar radio station with a report about the last question he was asked: "Will your mom have a nice hot meal ready for you when you get home?" Gender stereotypes are very slow to die.

I lost decisively on November 6, 58–42 percent. Though defeat stung, it was expected. What was not was how narrowly Walter Mondale carried his home state, and how comparatively few Minnesotans turned out in the 1984 election. Mondale's winning margin in Minnesota was just 3,761 votes. Minnesota was the only state he carried, and he had to make an extraordinary statewide effort in the campaign's closing days to make sure he did. That effort was of no help to me and other DFLers. The DFL lost control of the Minnesota House in that election. And though the state's turnout again led the nation, it was the second-lowest in a presidential election since Minnesota started keeping such records in 1950. That was astonishing, considering the stakes for Minnesota in the possibility of installing one of its own in the White House.

As I conceded defeat at the St. Paul Civic Center on election night, I took the long view. I asserted that history would prove me right on issues like arms control, Social Security protection, and a constitutional guarantee of equal rights for women. Then I spoke for the state's women: "Our time has come. Not this day, to be sure. But we have arrived. In the long history of Minnesota, dozens and dozens of men have run for the United States Senate. Half of them have been defeated. Though never elected, only two women have run. I will not be the last."[27]

It took another twenty-two years for Minnesota to elect its first female US senator, Amy Klobuchar.

Modernizing Democracy

I returned to the secretary of state's office in November 1984, exhausted and in debt but not in despair. To have run and lost an election is not an awful thing. I was still in public office, still engaged in important work that I loved. And I was buoyed by headlines like the one in the *St. Paul Pioneer Press* two days after the election: "Growe Is Winner in Women's Cause." I heard much the same thing repeatedly in the weeks following the election. Just running the full race with dignity and courage had been a breakthrough for women, I was assured. Gender barriers are stubborn things; they don't fall quickly. Of the ten women who ran for the US Senate in 1984, the only winner was Republican incumbent Nancy Landon Kassebaum of Kansas.[1]

Other women would follow, and I would be there to encourage them. Outreach and advice to female candidates and officeholders—in both parties, in Minnesota, and around the country—were priorities for me from the start of my political career. They've remained priorities ever since. I count as my mentees scores of women who've held elective office in the past forty years.

I was eager to get back to work in the secretary of state's office. But I could not say no when the Democratic Senate Campaign Committee invited me to Washington, DC, a few months after the election to debrief the women who led advocacy organizations that had been helpful to my campaign. Those women had considered me the female Senate challenger with the best shot in the nation, yet I'd lost by 16 percentage points. They asked, what more could they have done? I offered them a lengthy analysis of my defeat that included some self-criticism. For example, I said, I could have or should have hired senior staffers with more Senate campaign experience and could have or should have settled earlier on a simple message and stayed with it.[2]

I emphasized two points. One: gender bias is real and ought not be minimized or wished away. Women candidates are held to a double standard, and should counsel each other to expect as much and respond effectively. "When I was heated, it was read as shrill. When I was touching, it read 'emotional.' When I was committed, then I was simple. When I was perplexed, then I could not comprehend," I told the group. I had learned, and others must, that to succeed where no woman has succeeded before, a female candidate must be twice as prepared and work twice as hard as her male opponent.

My second big point was about money. I had been outspent four to one. "There's more than a little truth in the notion that there was nothing wrong with my campaign that $3 million wouldn't cure," I said. "No single factor had greater weight than money" in determining the election's outcome. Sexism colored how the money difference between Boschwitz and me was interpreted, I added. No Minnesota pundit faulted Boschwitz's money advantage. I suspect it was simply assumed that a woman running for an office traditionally held by men would be unable to keep up financially.

My recommendation was more early money from national advocacy groups and individuals, spent to defeat targeted incumbents. "Without it, these races are over before they begin," I advised. Among those who heard me that day was Ellen Malcolm, a savvy former White House communications aide in the Carter administration. She took my words to heart. A few weeks later, she invited like-minded friends to a meeting in her basement and asked them to bring their Rolodexes. That meeting founded EMILY's List—an acronym for Early Money Is Like Yeast (because it raises dough). More than thirty years later, EMILY's List has raised and spent more than $600 million to elect pro-choice Democratic women to office, and has contributed to the election of twenty-six Democratic women to the US Senate.[3]

I saw that running for the Senate had raised my profile, both nationally and at home. It had given me visibility and credibility that I had previously lacked in some quarters. Those were assets that I resolved to apply to my work as secretary of state. The office needed

I remained active in women's issues. At a 1991 pro-choice rally, I appeared with Joan Mondale (front left), Marlene Johnson (front right), Kathleen Vellenga (middle right), and Nancy Brataas (back, with glasses). Verna Pitts

*My children nominated me for secretary of state at the DFL state convention,
June 1986. Michael and Colleen are at left; I'm leaning on David.*

modernization; election law recodification was not yet finished; and
turnout, though higher than in other states, could be improved. That
work deserved my attention, I decided. I let it be known that I would
run for reelection as secretary of state in 1986, and I mentally set aside
suggestions that I should try again in 1988 or beyond for the Senate
or some other office somebody else deemed important. The work of
my office was important, to me and to democracy.

• • •

I had a great team to help me. It's ironic that one of the best hires we
ever made started work a few days before the 1984 DFL state convention, while my full attention wasn't on operations in the State Office
Building. Office manager Tom Durand, whom we hired in 1978, and
deputy secretary Elaine Voss took the lead in hiring Joe Mansky. His
first title was elections procedures advisor; by 1988, he was elections
director. He was thirty years old in 1984, a native of the Chicago area,
an environmental sciences manager by training, and a hydrologist for
the Missouri River Basin Commission before that office was abolished
by President Ronald Reagan in 1981. He had data management skills

but no experience in elections. We thought we were taking a chance with him, but the number-two position in the elections division had been vacant for months and we simply could not leave it unfilled any longer. When Joe retired thirty-five years later as elections manager for Ramsey County, he was widely seen as one of the nation's leading authorities on election administration. In Minnesota, he's legendary.[4]

Joe's hiring could be a case study of the role serendipity plays in employment practices. Mansky says he came to Minnesota in 1982 because it was a good place to ski. He didn't have a job in hand and didn't find much that suited his skills and background. While filling a temporary job for Hennepin County, he sent us a résumé and promptly forgot that he had done so. When we wrote back, he thought we had sent him a fundraising letter and disregarded it. When we finally reached him, he agreed to a job interview three days later. He spent the night before the interview studying Minnesota election law at the University of Minnesota Law Library. Joe has a steel-trap memory. He dazzled us with his ability to cite chapter and verse about state election law.

When he started work on June 4, I was out campaigning, naturally. Joe says he saw so little of me those first months that he began to wonder if I knew who he was. If I didn't then, I soon would.

Minnesota's state voter registration requirement was ten years old in 1984. Election Day registration had been grudgingly accepted by most of the county auditors and city elections clerks who made it work. But very little else was uniform about the way Minnesotans voted then. Not all counties had preregistration; some thought Election Day registration was adequate. Some rural counties didn't have sufficient staffing to keep a registration window open at the courthouse throughout the business day.

Most polling places in the state were not supplied with lists of registered voters, as they are now. Such lists didn't exist. Voters typically signed in by filling out a postcard. Around the state, three means of casting ballots were in use: lever machines in the large cities, computer punch cards in mid-sized cities and suburbs, and paper ballots in rural areas. The error rate with punch cards and paper ballots was estimated at five of every one thousand ballots—an unacceptably high level. Absentee ballots were rejected at a still higher rate, and practices for handling them varied widely. How results were reported to the secretary of state's office and, ultimately, the State Canvassing Board, which certifies results after an election, was also variable. Some counties relied on the US mail. In one memorable case, we sent the state patrol to far-northwestern Marshall County to pick up the official results for the canvassing board.

To Joe's dismay, he found that nothing concerning elections in my office had yet been computerized. In fact, the only computer in the entire office was an IBM PC XT (an early personal computer) that Joe found unused and stashed in a corner. (Home computers were just becoming common in the 1980s, and government offices are rarely early adopters of new technology.) Voter registration and recording had been computerized in some Minnesota election offices then, including St. Paul, Minneapolis, and Duluth, but each of those places operated with its own software. Their databases could not be easily combined. Seven counties had no permanent system of voter registration at all. Many counties still kept records on handwritten postcards stored in bulging file drawers.

That's just what my office's corporate division was doing when I took the reins in the 1970s. Everything the office did then required a paper record. Often, that record consisted of a three-by-five-inch card, filed alphabetically and retained for the next sixty or seventy years. I remember being astonished by the scene in the office the first time I watched our corporate staff at work. All day, they took telephone calls from entrepreneurs asking whether the name they wanted to give their new corporation was still available or already in use. We had a half dozen or more phones in the office, each with a long cord that allowed a staffer to move from cabinet to cabinet to search for the caller's proposed business name. The recipe cards were in metal file drawers that were purportedly moisture-proof. But after a few decades, the cards tended to stick together, making the staffers' searches difficult and testing the callers' patience. During busy periods, phone cords would become hopelessly tangled.

I was eager to find a better way. Tom Durand started the move away from paper records in the office's corporate division after he became office manager in 1978. (He likes to say that when he arrived, the office's most modern piece of equipment was its one electric typewriter—and that the supply cabinet still contained ink for fountain pens.) But the move wasn't initially to digital records; it was to microfiche. While that was superior to all those sticky cards, it was still slow and awkward to use. Soon after Joe arrived, Tom and Joe were discussing how computers could improve our operation.

Within a few months, Joe was using our one and only computer to collect and tabulate the September 11 primary vote records for the canvassing board. Later, when we needed more computing capacity than we had, we arranged to take our data and enter it on a computer at State Planning Agency offices across the capitol complex.

It was a modest start to something big. Joe, Tom, Elaine, and I saw that everything the office did ought to be digitized as soon as possible, in both the corporate and elections divisions. We started with the corporate records, ending for good both the old three-by-five cards and the microfiche records that had replaced them not long before. It was a significant improvement. Now staffers could access information without leaving the terminals at their desks, and a searchable database could be shared with law firms and banks who make frequent use of the information we archived.

Tom turned next to computerizing the Uniform Commercial Code files. Those are records lenders file documenting any non–real estate fixtures or equipment against which their business customers have borrowed money. Those records are in turn checked by future lenders before they allow borrowers to use fixtures or equipment as collateral, so potential borrowers cannot use the same items for multiple loans. Computerizing and centralizing those records in a statewide database was a first in the nation and a boon to lenders, quickly giving them up-to-date information about liened property for any borrower in the state.

• • •

Something small that Joe spotted during his first election season became significant later. A state House race in New Hope, a Minneapolis suburb, was won by DFLer Ann Rest over Independent-Republican representative Dorothy Hokr by only sixty votes. Any federal, state, or legislative race decided by a margin of less than 0.5 percentage points qualifies for an automatic recount under Minnesota law. Joe was dispatched to New Hope to preside over the recount process, and in so doing he noticed that the punch card ballot pages that the district used were designed in a confusing manner. It would be easy for a voter to punch the wrong hole without realizing his or her error. These were butterfly ballots, which became notorious in Florida in the hotly contested 2000 presidential election. He also saw that when punch card ballots were handled multiple times, as they are in a recount, perforated paper bits, called chads, can be inadvertently dislodged from the cards. That leaves the appearance that the voter cast votes for more than one candidate, thus spoiling the ballot for recount purposes.[5]

When Joe reported his concerns to me, I took several steps to remedy the situation. First, I decided to stop certifying new punch card voting equipment for use in state elections. We were the first state in the country to do so. That didn't end their use immediately. But it meant that as equipment became outdated and needed to be replaced, punch cards would be phased out. In 1990, punch card voting was still in use in 18 percent of the state's precincts. The last use of a punch card system in Minnesota was in the city of Biwabik in 1994. All punch cards were gone well before *hanging chads* became household words in 2000.[6]

Second, I also decided to ask the legislature to prohibit the use of any new voting system in Minnesota that lacked a paper ballot, including the then-emerging touch-screen voting systems. We wanted the verifiability that paper provides. Again, we were the first in the nation to take that step. Third, I instructed Joe to revise the administrative rules for use of the punch card system to eliminate the butterfly ballot format from further use in Minnesota elections. Butterfly ballots flew away in Minnesota fifteen years before the *Bush v. Gore* controversy in Florida.

Punch cards were still in use in 1986 when what Joe calls his craziest election crisis occurred. A big thunderstorm socked Rice County, south of the Twin Cities, not long after the polls closed on primary

Election Day that year. County officials had packed the ballots in an unsealed metal box and hauled them in an open-box pickup truck to the courthouse, where they were to be tabulated by the county's computer. When the box was opened, officials found that several hundred punched ballots were wet and would potentially jam the computer. They called Joe.

"Put the wet cards in the microwave to dry them," he recommended, not at all sure the trick would work. It did, and Joe's reputation as an election wizard grew.

Securing the accuracy not only of the initial count but also of any subsequent recount was a high priority in our office. Close elections that trigger automatic recounts are not uncommon in Minnesota. The state has seen eighty-eight recounts in legislative races since 1849. It has the distinction of being home to the closest gubernatorial election in US history, DFLer Karl Rolvaag's defeat of Republican governor Elmer L. Andersen by ninety-one votes in 1962. More recently, US senator Al Franken defeated US senator Norm Coleman by 312 votes in 2008, in a contest that featured the largest recount in US history. Both of those squeaker elections led to months of recounting and litigation. Through much of its history, Minnesota has been well served by two vigorous parties that compete on a fairly even basis in large portions of the state. Gerrymandering for the sake of maximizing the number of so-called safe seats for the two parties has been rare.[7]

State law specifies that recounts must be done by hand, not machine—a provision enacted at Joe's and my request, based on our less-than-satisfactory experience with the earliest optical scan recounts in the mid-1980s. That requirement means that the ballots on which votes are cast must be legible to human as well as electronic eyes. And it means that the count must be replicable, at multiple times and places if necessary. That requirement colored our thinking every time new voting technology became available.

Joe and I were fans of the optical scanning equipment that was first used in Minnesota in the 1985 Minnetonka city election, and as a test case in the 1986 state election in Brooklyn Park. Optical scanners brought several advantages. They produced a paper trail. A scanned ballot could easily be examined and understood by volunteers in a recount. In the event of a power failure (Joe remembered that Rice County thunderstorm), voting could continue. The ballots could be held for machine scanning when power was restored, or simply counted by hand. Voters liked the sense of security they got from inserting their ballots into the counting machine directly, without any intermediary action by an election judge. Older voters in Minneapolis and St. Paul, where lever machines had been used for decades, told us they appreciated being able to again hold their ballots in their hands.

Further, if scanners were installed at every polling place, ballot errors could be immediately detected. Voters would know right away that they had marked their ballot in a manner that made it invalid, and could try again. That wasn't a small thing in Minnesota. In the 1986 state primary election, in which both parties waged spirited fights over their respective nominations for governor, I was appalled when our projection from sample precincts found that nine percent of the ballots cast had been spoiled by voters' attempts to vote in both parties' primaries. Nine percent of the vote in that primary was sixty-eight thousand votes, which in Minnesota is more than enough to determine the outcome of a lot of state elections.

One obvious remedy would be party registration, allowing voters access only to the primary ballot of their preregistered party. But that idea ran contrary to the tradition of openness and fluidity in democracy that Minnesotans prized—and it would mean that voters who preferred to keep their party preference private would be "outed" to election administrators and potentially to their neighbors. I knew well how my dad would have resisted the possibility that his hardware store customers would see his name on a partisan list. Party registration was not politically feasible in Minnesota, I told reporters at the State Canvassing Board meeting on September 23, 1986, that certified the primary results. Tactics like better ballot or voting equipment design would be needed to bring down the error rate. I explained that the best remedy I knew was adoption of optical-scan voting machines that can immediately identify errors and give voters a chance to correct them. Election officials in Minneapolis and St. Paul evidently were listening. They switched from lever machines to optical scanners for their city elections the next year. Within a decade, the entire state had converted to this superior voting technology, which remains in use today.[8]

• • •

The other error-prone element in Minnesota's voting system was absentee voting. Too many absentee ballots were never counted simply because they were returned too late. Others were disqualified because voters did not carefully follow instructions. In addition, there was a dirty secret in some precincts: absentee ballots weren't counted because of the time and effort required to count them by hand. They were long paper ballots, still in use at a time when hand counting on election night was becoming rare. The ballots were delivered directly to the polling places by the postal service, where election judges were required to process and count them late in a long and tiring day.

The federal government gave us our first nudge toward improvement. Minnesota law had said that absentee ballots could be obtained no earlier than twenty days before an election. That didn't pass muster with the feds, who wanted a thirty-day window to better serve military personnel. Minnesota was sued by the federal government to lengthen its absentee ballot window. As a stopgap measure, we agreed that we would accept and count ballots from overseas and military voters received up to ten days after the election. In 1985, the legislature gave us a better remedy by allowing the start of absentee balloting thirty days before the election.

That began what would become several decades of intermittent tussles over absentee ballot policies in Minnesota. The issues would outlast my tenure in the secretary of state's office. I wanted to make absentee voting easier for what I considered completely nonpartisan reasons. If democracy is to live up to its promise of inclusive self-governance, it needs to allow for easy voting by people of all ages and in all stages of life. Not everyone can appear in person at a neighborhood polling station on a specific day between specific hours. Their reasons are varied—and in my view, it is not government's role to judge some reasons more legitimate than others. State law then restricted absentee voting to people who were willing to sign a sworn statement that they would be absent from their home precincts on Election Day, or were incapacitated with an illness or disability, or were prevented from voting by religious observances, or were serving as an election judge in a polling place other than their own. "We are encouraging our citizens to lie," I told legislators as I began pushing for elimination of the sworn-statement requirement.

I also asked the legislature to allow for mail balloting–only elections—which, in essence, are a version of absentee voting—in sparsely populated regions of the state. The positive reception of that idea in 1987 gave me a false sense that no-excuses absentee voting wouldn't be far behind. In those years, Republicans believed that absentee voting disproportionately benefited their candidates. GOP candidates' promotion of the option to cast an early ballot via absentee voting had worked to their advantage in other states, they believed. For example, California Republican governor George Deukmejian won his office in 1982 on the strength of a strong showing among absentee voters. (Rudy Boschwitz would try that tactic in Minnesota in 1990, with less evident success.) The Republican view then was that while Election Day registration likely benefited Democrats, readily available absentee voting was a plus for Republicans. On the basis of that tenuous balance, bipartisan deals could be struck and bad ideas struck down. For example, Independent-Republican representative Craig Shaver of Wayzata got nowhere in 1985 with his bill to restrict the number of nonregistered voters for whom an already-registered voter in a precinct could vouch on Election Day—that is, could sign a statement attesting to knowledge that the registrant lived in the precinct. His bill failed to get out of a Republican-controlled committee when rural members of his own party resisted the change. But the desire of some Minnesota Republicans to make Election Day registration more difficult would prove persistent.[9]

Regardless of party, legislators are reluctant to embrace any change in voting procedures. They all consider themselves experts on elections, and they are typically satisfied with the way the current procedures worked for them. When I recommended any change, I knew it was my obligation to sell legislators on its advantages—and the only advantages they valued were ones that accrued to either voters in general or them in particular. Arguing that a proposed change would save money never packed the same punch.

That's why my pitch for voting by mail was that people wanted it and liked it where it had been tried elsewhere, in Oregon, Washington, California, and Montana. I argued that voting only at the polls placed a burden on people in remote rural areas, many of whom had to drive long distances and either arrange for child care or bring restless small children with them. That burden helped explain low voter turnout in local elections in a state that otherwise led the nation in election turnout, I argued.

The 1987 legislature agreed to let us give voting by mail a try. We had an eighteen-month experimental window to allow local jurisdictions to conduct entire elections by mail—but only in elections involving ballot questions, not candidates. A separate measure allowed Greater Minnesota municipalities with populations of fewer than four hundred registered voters to conduct a state, federal, or local election by mail—an option technically called mail balloting. Luverne, a city of about forty-five hundred in the state's southwestern corner, was the first to try an all-mail election for a city charter change, one that had already been rejected by voters in a low-turnout election in March. Ballots were mailed in mid-August to try to pass the charter revision again. When the votes were counted on September 1, the change had been approved decisively. That turnabout was not what made state headlines, however. Rather, it was that voter participation went from 238 in the March election to 1,469 in the all-mail election. That turnout boost got wide attention and editorial praise. The first county all-mail election was in far-northern Lake of the Woods County in June 1988. The mail balloting option remains available today, though in a more limited fashion than I would have preferred.[10]

I was wrong to think that with voting by mail in place, "no-excuses" absentee voting would soon win the legislature's favor. It took twenty-two years! The legislature finally accepted my 1991 proposal in 2013. The delay had much to do with a change in sentiment about absentee voting and voting by mail among Republicans. In the 1980s and 1990s, anti-abortion forces solidified their control of the Minnesota

Republican Party. Those forces weren't keen on allowing a larger share of the state's votes to be cast before Election Day. One of their favorite campaign tactics was to blitz the parking lots of like-minded churches with flyers on the weekend before an election (preferably, in their playbook, after parishioners had heard a fiery anti-abortion sermon). We were told that resistance from the anti-abortion lobby led to Republican pressure on Governor Arne Carlson to veto our no-excuses absentee voting bill in 1994. Carlson, who supported abortion rights, was already on the outs with his party as he faced a tough re-election fight. He needed Republican legislators to stand with him to uphold his many vetoes of DFL-sponsored bills. Though I met with the governor personally to make the case for the change, Carlson bowed to pressure and vetoed our bill. As he did, he announced a rule he would henceforth follow when deciding the fate of bills related to elections: he would only sign into law the elections bills that the legislature had approved with broad bipartisan support. That rule was so well received that it was adopted by all four of his successors to date—one independent, one Republican, and two DFLers. I can't fault those governors' bipartisan intentions. But Carlson's rule has made election reform harder to achieve.[11]

GOP opposition further hardened in 1996 after the nation's first all-mail US Senate election in Oregon. It produced a narrow, upset victory for Democratic US representative Ron Wyden over Republican Gordon Smith, a leader in that state's legislature. The *Washington Post* said the election's "mail-in voting process was deemed an unqualified success" because it produced a higher turnout than recent conventional elections had. But that success was in the eye of the beholder, and many eyes increasingly viewed anything pertaining to elections through a partisan lens.[12]

● ● ●

The computerization of the secretary of state's election operations that Joe Mansky and Tom Durand began in a small way in 1984 gained speed every year thereafter. With my encouragement, that work got a push from the legislature in 1987. Our office was directed to "develop and implement a statewide computerized voter registration system to facilitate voter registration and provide a central data base containing voter registration information from around the state. The system must be accessible to the county auditor of each county in the state." We had an inkling about the origin of that last sentence. We'd been told that the Senate's most powerful member, DFL majority leader Roger Moe, had been appalled during the 1986 campaign year when he realized that in many parts of the state, DFL Senate candidates could not go to a county auditor's office and obtain a printout of all of the registered voters in the county. That year, there were thirty-three different computer-based voter registration systems used in Minnesota, and eighteen counties still had no computerized voter lists at all. Moe wanted his candidates to have those lists in hand when senators were next on the ballot, in 1990.[13]

We did too. But we didn't know how to stretch the meager $1.5 million the legislature provided for this purpose as far as was needed. By then, our office had the computer hardware necessary to build a statewide voter registration system. Many counties already had the needed equipment, but for eighteen of them, the computer we supplied would be their very first. It was up to us to see that the auditors' offices in every county had a computer terminal that could be linked with the statewide network, plus a dot matrix printer for distributing voter lists. Digital distribution was a thing of the future. We would also have to develop standardized software and go on the road to train county officials to work with the new system.

A point of contention with the counties that had already entered the computer age was whether they could keep their existing databases and periodically upload them to the state's system, rather than replacing their existing systems with the state's. We made some county officials unhappy by insisting that a statewide database would better comply with the law's requirements and meet the state's needs. It would allow officials processing a new registration from someone who had moved to quickly discover whether that voter was already registered elsewhere in the state, and allow for the immediate deletion of the voter's previous registration. The result was less duplication and more accuracy in voter rolls. It also allowed curious politicians to see a voter's entire voting history in the state, not just the voting history associated with his or her current registration.

At the same time that we were developing the statewide registration system, we were processing a surge in voter preregistration. At our urging, the 1987 legislature ordered that voter registration forms be distributed to Minnesotans along with income tax and motor vehicle registration forms, documents most Minnesotans receive from state government each year. The idea was soon dubbed "motor voter." In addition, the new law required state agencies that deal directly with the public to make voter registration forms consistently available. The result was two hundred thousand more new voters on the rolls before the 1988 election than were preregistered in 1986.[14]

It was a tremendous amount of work, for which Joe deserves great credit. He still laughs about some of the calls and questions he received from election administrators who were being introduced to computers for the first time. One county official called to complain that the new machine he had just received did not work.

"Check to see that it's plugged in," Joe advised. A long pause followed.

Finally, a response: "It works! The cord was still in the box."

We managed to get a bare-bones, twenty-county voter registration system up and running by the next year, 1988. It would take another election cycle before all eighty-seven counties' voter registration lists were connected and standardized. "Right now, there are 87 different ways of doing this," Tom Durand told *Star Tribune* reporter Gregor Pinney early in 1988. Henceforward, "there will be a standard way."[15]

We were breaking new ground. No other state had developed an online, real-time, statewide voter registration database. It didn't take long for other secretaries of state to take notice. Soon, curious visitors from other states began calling on our office to see for themselves what we were up to. And Tom Durand was invited to the John F. Kennedy School of Government at Harvard University to tell a conference about our project.

• • •

That wasn't the only big leap we made into modern telecommunications in 1988. The presidency was up for grabs in the 1988 election, and Minnesota's precinct caucuses were set for February 23—not the earliest in the nation but early enough to assure that multicandidate races would still be in progress in both major parties. The national spotlight would fall on the state's caucuses, if only for a few days. I didn't want the next-day story from Minnesota's caucuses to be something like, "Tens of thousands of Minnesotans went to meetings last night, and we'll know what they did in a few months," when the parties would finally elect national convention delegates. I thought it important that we be able to report caucus results a few hours after caucuses adjourn. That's what Minnesotans expect on election nights, I reasoned, and caucuses should be no different. Reporting results as soon as possible builds interest and participation in caucuses and, in turn, in voting. Why not ask the parties to conduct an unofficial tally of the presidential preferences of the delegates to county-unit conventions elected at the caucuses, and telephone the secretary of state's office with those results? One volunteer caller per precinct was all that would be needed on the local level. We would arrange for the telephone lines and computer technology to tabulate and disseminate the results. The Unisys computer company donated both hardware and staff to help us, and news organizations helped cover the costs.

Pulling this off involved clearing more than logistical hurdles. Major interference arose from an unexpected source, the Democratic National Committee. Minnesota's caucuses had been set by the state legislature for February 23, a date two weeks earlier than desired by the Democratic National Committee. In exchange for the national party's acceptance of Minnesota's date, DFL officials had promised to not release the results of their own survey of caucus participants' presidential preferences for two weeks. The DFL was free to make that deal with its own data, Elaine Voss and I told reporters. But it was not binding on the straw poll we'd planned, nor on the news organizations that were paying for the system we designed. We refused to back down—and two weeks before the caucuses, the Democratic National Committee did.[16]

"It was a formidable undertaking, and it worked," the *Star Tribune* reported the morning after the caucuses, in an edition whose front page featured a color photo of me, telephone pressed to my ear, taking a report on results. TV and newspaper reporters from across the country joined us that night to witness the results being reported. The *Star Tribune* said that by 11:20 PM, we had received fifty-four hundred telephone reports of caucus results, with the phones still ringing with more. Already at that hour, we had reports from three-fourths of Independent-Republican caucuses (where Kansas senator Robert Dole was Minnesotans' favorite) and two-thirds of DFL caucuses (where the eventual Democratic nominee that year, Massachusetts governor Michael Dukakis, had a good night). We earned editorial praise for producing the state's first-ever caucus-night reporting system, and I think we were due a share of credit for the boost in caucus attendance that year. Republican caucus attendance was nearly twice as large as it had been in 1984, and the DFL gain wasn't far behind.[17]

That success whetted our appetites for a more ambitious undertaking. We became aware that no secretary of state's office in the nation offered real-time, statewide results on election night. That meant that there was no centralized source for a reliable count as votes were tabulated. News organizations and political parties in Minnesota and most other states had cobbled together their own systems involving a mixture of real-time results and projections based on exit polling in sample precincts. In Minnesota, the Associated Press, serving all of the state's major newspapers and broadcast news outlets, had taken the lead for many years and charged their members for the costs. In addition, the *Star Tribune* employed a "100-precinct model" developed by University of Minnesota political scientist Charles Backstrom. These arrangements were costly for the news organizations and occasionally led to inaccurate projections and embarrassing headlines. News executives cheered us on as we set out to develop our own computer-based election-results reporting system. But—prudently—they didn't abandon their usual system in 1988. We needed to prove ourselves before they would bet their election coverage on us.

As Joe describes that hectic summer and fall in our office, "we were breaking new ground every time we came to work." With no model from another state to follow, it was a learn-as-you-go process. We were handicapped by the limited reach of our computer network. It was the same one that we were building for voter registration, and that would not reach every county in the state for another few years. But our good results with volunteer reporting from precinct caucuses emboldened us to try.[18]

The result of our efforts on election night were not spectacular. But neither were they disastrous. Our tally was consistently several hours behind that reported by the Associated Press. We were hampered by a slow system that would grind to a halt if too many people tried to input data at the same time. Elaine Voss and I had to get on the phone with some counties and ask them to hold off attempting to file their results for ten, twenty, or thirty minutes because the system was too busy. The patience of the tired people on the other end of the line was a tribute to their devotion to a well-run democracy. Elaine and I promised them and the reporters who met with us the next day that we would be ready with a more robust computer system before the next election.[19]

We made good on that promise. Little did we know that computers would be the least of our worries in 1990.

• • •

While I never took any election for granted, my reelection campaigns in 1982, 1986, and 1990 did not require heavy political exertion. I defeated three little-known Independent-Republican opponents by garnering 59 percent of the vote in 1982, 66 percent in 1986, and 62 percent in 1990.

But the theme on which my 1982 opponent campaigned stuck in a lot of Minnesotans' minds through the remainder of that decade. Mark Hanson, a twenty-five-year-old whose professional experience consisted of working on the staffs of Republican elected officials in Minnesota and Washington, told voters that the office of secretary of state should be eliminated. He argued that the work of the office was largely clerical and could be adequately performed by other state agencies, whose leaders are appointed by the governor.[20]

That flawed idea was mentioned repeatedly for years thereafter, and for a time seemed to be accepted as almost inevitable. For example, *Minneapolis Star and Tribune* columnist Jim Klobuchar—the father of Minnesota's current US senator—offered this casual aside in a column about me in 1985: "The office she holds today will eventually dissolve, provoking a musical-chairs scramble when the reorganization comes." That year, a bill was introduced in the legislature for a constitutional amendment to combine three elected state offices— auditor, treasurer, and secretary of state—into one. It got a flurry of attention before it eventually died.[21]

Then came the bizarre gubernatorial election of 1990. The events of that year made a clear case for keeping the state's chief election officer accountable to the voters, and no one else. Since then, the notion that Minnesota's democracy would be just fine without an independently elected secretary of state has died a deserved death.

DFL governor Rudy Perpich sought an unprecedented fourth term in 1990, and though his popularity had slipped from its peak, he was politically healthy enough to overcome a serious primary challenge from a future state attorney general, Mike Hatch. The Independent-Republican Party's nomination for governor was also decided with a primary, in which that party's increasingly dominant, religious-right faction flexed its muscle. GOP voters went with conservative business executive Jon Grunseth, who had never before held elective office, over the more moderate, three-term State Auditor Arne Carlson and four others. Grunseth topped Carlson by more than sixty thousand votes.[22]

A bomb went off in the race on October 15, three weeks and one day before the election. The *Star Tribune* reported that two women had signed sworn affidavits attesting to improper behavior by Grunseth at a 1981 home swimming pool party. They said he swam nude with them and attempted to remove their bathing suits; one said he tried to touch her breasts. The four young women reportedly involved were ages thirteen through sixteen and included Grunseth's stepdaughter. Grunseth denied the charges and accused Perpich of initiating them, a claim that was denied by both Perpich and the newspaper.[23]

While most IR Party officials stood by Grunseth in the ensuing days, a few party elders began talking about a replacement candidate. That's where I entered the drama. On October 17, in hopes of efficiently responding to the barrage of questions coming into my office, I summoned capitol reporters to a news conference to explain what state law requires in the event that a major party's candidate steps down before an election. I explained that the party in question would have a brief period—up to four days before the election—to designate an alternate candidate. If none were designated, the second-place finisher in the primary election—in this case, Arne Carlson—would become the party's candidate by default. In either case, my office would issue supplemental ballots for the governor's race—and the courts would likely have an emergency lawsuit on their hands, to iron out the several details about which the law was not clear.[24]

Carlson's supporters didn't wait for Grunseth to leave the race. Days after the swimming pool story broke, they initiated a write-in campaign. On October 22, Carlson embraced that effort as his own and said he was "in it to the end." That got me back into the saga. After consulting the attorney general's office, I informed county auditors that to be legitimate, a write-in vote for Carlson on the November 6 general election ballot must include the name of Carlson's little-known running mate, Red Wing mayor Joanell Dyrstad. Carlson went to the Minnesota Supreme Court on October 26 seeking a ruling that a write-in vote simply for him would be sufficient.[25]

But before the court could rule, another bomb exploded. The *Star Tribune* reported on October 28 that Grunseth had carried on a nine-year extramarital affair that spanned both of his marriages and had not ended until 1989, after his gubernatorial campaign began. Later that day—just nine days before the election—Grunseth announced his exit from the race. Two days later, the IR Party's central committee leaders announced that the party lacked an "appropriate committee" as required by state law to choose a replacement for Grunseth. That was an extraordinary move by the party's leaders, who ordinarily are loath to yield their power to choose candidates to anyone else. It meant that, by default, they were allowing Carlson's name to replace

Grunseth's on a supplemental ballot. Leaders of the IR executive committee evidently feared that a less-electable candidate would emerge if they took the matter to the full central committee.[26]

The next day, with that word in hand, I ordered that Carlson's name replace Grunseth's on the ballot. I added that with Carlson's name would be that of his candidate for lieutenant governor, Joanell Dyrstad, not Grunseth's running mate, Sharon Clark. "We have reached the conclusion that your candidacy for lieutenant governor is no longer operable in the absence of a gubernatorial candidate," I wrote to Clark. As I expected, Clark immediately filed a lawsuit. The very next day—November 1—the Minnesota Supreme Court sided with me in a 5–2 decision.[27]

Every move I made that tumultuous October was done after considerable consultation with state government's top election lawyers (including future US District Court chief judge John Tunheim), our in-house expert, Joe Mansky, and an attorney on our staff, Bert Black. I took pains to avoid any unconventional interpretation of the law that might appear to provide an undue advantage to either party or candidate. Of course, I was much aware that I, too, was on the 1990 ballot, seeking a fifth term. I was accountable to the voters, not to my party or my party's governor. Had Minnesota been a state in which the chief election officer is a gubernatorial appointee, the pressure on me that October would have been quite different, and quite uncomfortable.

Supreme Court chief justice Peter Popovich's dissent in the high court's 5–2 decision illustrated that it was possible to make more partisan choices. Popovich, who had been appointed by Rudy Perpich, argued that since, according to the state constitution, the candidates for governor and lieutenant governor run as a ticket, both of their withdrawals were necessary to remove their names from the ballot. Since Clark had not withdrawn, Popovich argued, Grunseth's name should still be on the ballot on November 6. Another possibility was presented in an amicus brief filed with the court by the DFL party's attorney, Alan Weinblatt. He argued that I had erred in allowing the IR Party to dodge the question, and that the court should order the IR Party's "appropriate committee" to name a candidate.[28]

Had I taken either of those positions, we still would have wound up in court, and the outcome might have been no different. But my reputation for nonpartisan election administration would have been badly damaged. Keeping Grunseth's name on the ballot would have been a boon to Rudy Perpich's reelection chances. An October 19–21 poll by the *Star Tribune* and KSTP-TV showed that Perpich would likely win both a matchup with Grunseth alone and a three-way race with both Grunseth and Carlson running. But in a head-to-head pairing, Carlson led Perpich by 10 percentage points. I was told that Perpich was furious when the court sided with me and kept Grunseth's name off the ballot. I did not experience his wrath directly. But Associate Justice Alexander M. "Sandy" Keith's decision to side with the court's majority rather than with Popovich—coming not long after Perpich had appointed Keith to be Popovich's successor as chief justice— caused a breach in Keith's thirty-year friendship with Perpich that was not repaired before Perpich died in 1995.[29]

Carlson defeated Perpich on November 6 by nearly sixty thousand votes, just under 4 percentage points. In the same election, Paul Wellstone unseated my 1984 nemesis Rudy Boschwitz. Turnout was 56 percent—not great, but better than I feared it would be as the Grunseth campaign came crashing down. And I quietly reveled in an exhausted public's sense that their election system had served them well. A letter to the editor in the *Star Tribune* echoed the plaudits I was hearing from around the state: "Secretary of State Joan Growe demonstrated that one can run on a partisan ticket and at the same time make decisions and carry out official duties in a manner that respects the opportunity for every Minnesotan, regardless of political persuasion, to vote. . . . Her actions were in the interest of all voters."[30]

CHAPTER

9

The Nation's Leader

If Minnesota's 1990 election had not made a splash (pardon the swimming pool pun) in other ways, it still might have been noticed by my peers around the country because of the voter turnout it generated. The US Census Bureau started keeping state turnout statistics in 1976. That timing makes it difficult to make the before-and-after comparisons that would show how Minnesota's shift to Election Day registration in 1974 affected its turnout rank among the states. But those figures say unambiguously that in every presidential and midterm election but one (1986) between 1976 and 1990, Minnesota's turnout led the nation. Among my fellow secretaries of state, I had become the spokesperson for the State That Votes.[1]

I had been active in the National Association of Secretaries of State (NASS) since my earliest days in office. A nonpartisan group founded in 1904, NASS seemed during my first few meetings to be largely populated by clubby, gray-haired men who had been in office for decades. They enjoyed their part-business, part-pleasure, twice-yearly meetings, one per year in Washington, DC, a second one in a host state. While in Washington, those elder secretaries might talk a little election law with members of Congress, but not in a way to make waves back home. They maintained that avoiding controversy was the key to political longevity.

Imagine their consternation, then, as a cohort of younger secretaries, including me, appeared and asked them to throw the organization's collective political weight behind some edgy ideas. Take the Equal Rights Amendment. In 1977, the National Organization for Women announced a boycott of the fifteen states that by then had

failed to ratify the amendment that would give women a constitutional guarantee of equal standing with men under the law. Colorado's Republican secretary of state, Mary Estill Buchanan, and I
thought that NASS should honor the boycott in future meetings. I
raised my hand at a plenary session and said, "I don't think we should
meet in any state that has not ratified the ERA." I then watched as
one of the organization's graybeards left his seat on the opposite side
of the room and slowly walked around the meeting hall to directly
address me. "You know, you're not supposed to say anything in these
meetings for the first few years that you're here," he scolded.

I paid his advice no heed. I considered NASS a useful forum for the
exchange of ideas about election policies and voting technology, and
I intended to make friends and get as much value as I could from the
association. Fortunately, each succeeding election brought more like-
minded secretaries to the group. And each succeeding election bur-
nished Minnesota's reputation as a state that does democracy right.

I was elected NASS's president in 1979. I was neither the youngest
person nor the first woman to hold that post. Nevertheless, I put a
fresh face on an organization with a tired image. I also took the post at
a time when secretaries of state were hearing growing concern about
a downward drift in US citizen participation in elections. Choosing a
Minnesotan may have been the organization's way of rewarding a
state that was bucking an unwelcome trend.[2]

To me, the key to Minnesota's turnout success was the smart move
the state made in 1973—Election Day registration. To be sure, Minnesota's New England and Scandinavian roots, its high educational
attainment, and its culture of civic engagement all help propel people
to the polls. Convenient polling locations and readily available absentee ballots help too. But voter awareness that preregistration is not
necessary in order to cast a ballot makes what I believe is the decisive
difference between Minnesota's election turnout compared to other
states. It's no coincidence that the other states that are consistently at
the top of voter-turnout rankings are Wisconsin, Maine, and Oregon,
which were also early adopters of Election Day registration.

I said as much to my NASS colleagues whenever I had the chance.
But I did not get very far. The idea that Americans should be on

a preapproved list before they can be trusted with a ballot is now nearly two centuries old. Preregistration, weeks or months before an election, still goes almost unquestioned in much of the country. My NASS colleagues were intrigued by what we were doing in Minnesota, but most weren't willing to push the idea in their home states. When Sherrod Brown, today a US senator, was secretary of state in Ohio in the mid-1980s, he invited me to testify about our experience before the Ohio legislature. It wasn't until 2005 that Ohio gave same-day registration a limited trial—but then scrapped it ten years later, when Republicans took full control of that state's legislature.[3]

My NASS connections led to a number of opportunities to tell Minnesota's voting success story. On four occasions, I was invited to testify before Congress. The first of those experiences was made memorable for me by the kindness of Vice President Walter Mondale, who showed up at the start of my committee appearance to introduce me. I saw little evidence that my testimony changed minds on most of those four occasions. Like their state-level counterparts, congressional committees that deal with election policies tend to be stacked with conservatives whose goal is to preserve the status quo. Similarly, I was invited to meet with the boards of directors of several national foundations whose missions included the promotion of democracy. They too listened politely, but were unwilling to take positions that might be seen as controversial or partisan.

Increasingly in the 1990s, easier voter registration fit both of those categories. I had long known that there was a partisan edge to resistance to Election Day registration. My Republican predecessor and several of my Independent-Republican opponents had made criticism of Election Day registration a campaign theme. Yet in Minnesota through the 1980s, both parties gave at least lip-service support to making it easier for people to vote.

An indication that the GOP nationally had lost interest in easier registration came in 1993 when the so-called motor voter bill came to the US Senate. It would make voter registration forms available at a variety of government service outlets, including motor vehicle registration stations, and allow registrants to complete and submit the voting forms at those agencies. The concept was modeled after the

law my office had pushed through the Minnesota Legislature in 1987.
Minnesota US senator Dave Durenberger, a Republican, was an early
supporter of the motor voter concept, and in 1992—when Republican
George H. W. Bush was president—it appeared that Durenberger had
plenty of Republican company on the issue. But Bush vetoed the 1992
bill, and in 1993, with Democrat Bill Clinton in the White House, Republican support for the motor voter idea melted away. Five Senate
moderates, including Durenberger, were of little help when the bill
returned to the floor that spring. They bowed to their party's pressure
and demanded that a number of weakening amendments be added
to the bill. Senate Majority Leader George Mitchell, a Democrat,
was willing to do something seldom seen in today's Washington. He
agreed to their requests in order to win their votes and give the final product a bipartisan veneer. I testified on the bill in Washington.
While I was disappointed by the Republican senators' action, I was
honored to be present at the White House Rose Garden on May 20

*With Michigan Secretary of State Richard H. Austin and President Bill Clinton at
the signing of the Motor Voter Act in the Rose Garden, May 20, 1993*

when President Bill Clinton signed the National Voter Registration Act of 1993, also known as the Motor Voter Act.[4]

• • •

The attention paid to Minnesota's 1987 motor voter bill as Congress assembled its own version likely added to my state's reputation as a place that "does elections right." It may have been among the reasons that, beginning in 1990, I was invited to join teams of election observers at far-flung places around the globe. I made seven such trips, starting in Romania in 1990 and ending in Yemen in 2003. Some of those trips were arranged under the auspices of the United Nations; others were the work of the National Democratic Institute (NDI), a nongovernmental organization founded in 1983 that's devoted to strengthening democracy around the world and on whose board of directors I eventually served. Among its board members today are former secretary of state Madeleine Albright and former vice president Walter Mondale. NDI's president in 1990 was J. Brian Atwood, whom I had come to know well when he was the top staffer at the Democratic Senate Campaign Committee in 1984. Atwood would go on to serve a stint as dean of the Humphrey Institute (now School) of Public Affairs at the University of Minnesota, where I am a member of the advisory council.[5]

Those trips signified something that Americans ought to appreciate. In the eyes of the United Nations and much of the free world, a nation's ability to conduct fair and free elections is an indicator of its potential for stability and prosperity. If a young nation can pull off an election without coercion or intimidation of voters, mishandling of ballots, or manipulation of results, that nation is seen by wealthier nations as worthy of assistance. Both in money and reputation, much was riding on the reports we observers made.

The teams of fifteen to twenty people chosen to be election observers were all well versed in election administration or law, though few others had been secretaries of US states. Before each trip, teams spent several days immersed in briefings about the country we would visit and the circumstances of the coming election. Teams traveled together, then split into pairs upon arrival and scattered to chosen

As a United Nations elections observer in Yemen, 2003

polling sites around the country. Each pair would watch the balloting and chat with voters and election judges for thirty to forty-five minutes per location, then move on to another site. The days were long. Sometimes we visited more than a dozen polling places per day, occasionally returning to the same place twice. Our strict orders were to be observers, nothing more. If we saw irregularities, we were to note them but not try to correct them on the spot. Our safety was a priority.

The trips were challenging, yet exhilarating. My first, in May 1990, was to witness the election in Romania after the overthrow and assassination of communist dictator Nicolae Ceaușescu the previous

December. It was that nation's first free election since 1937. Our particular concern was the treatment of Romania's Romani population, an ethnic minority that comprises a share of that nation's population estimated at between 3 and 12 percent. We heard and duly recorded a number of complaints about how they had been treated. That election's lopsided outcome raised more suspicions. Ion Iliescu, a former Communist Party official who had been the nation's leader since the December coup, won with an overwhelming 85 percent of the vote, a credulity-straining result in a multicandidate race. Nevertheless, the US State Department announced a week later that while "serious distortions marked the Romanian electoral process," in its judgment, the election had been "generally free."[6]

I came home from that first experience eager to tell Minnesotans about the Romanians' determination to participate—they often stood in line for three hours in order to vote—and their pride in reviving democracy. A somewhat indelicate personal experience illustrates how eager they were to welcome us. During our visits to polling places, I had an urgent need to visit a bathroom. All that was available at the rural outpost that was serving as a polling place was an outhouse. I set out to visit that little building, only to be stopped by the head election judge. This won't do, he explained to my driver and interpreter. You must go to the priest's house, several blocks away. You are our important guest. You must have a flush toilet, and the priest has the only one in town. Off I went, trailed by my driver and two or three others. The priest was more than accommodating. When I emerged from his bathroom, I was met with a bouquet of flowers and an invitation to join the priest for tea. How could I refuse? Of course, tea time left me with another urgent need for a bathroom break. Once again, the proud villagers insisted that only the best toilet in town would do for a woman who had come all the way from America to watch them vote. The priest obliged me again before I left.[7]

My third trip as an election observer made the deepest impression on me. I feel so privileged to have witnessed South Africa's first post-apartheid election—the first in which all adult citizens, regardless of race, had the right to vote. The election was a four-day affair, April 26–29, 1994. I was there from April 20 to May 1 under United

Nations auspices, wearing a clearly marked vest that itself became a matter of concern. We were advised not to wear our blue vests in one of the cities we visited. The UN's familiar round map emblem on the back of the vests presented snipers with an easy target, we were told.

When we stayed in the nation's largest and most modern city, Johannesburg, we were advised that violence was a possibility. That possibility became real after we visited the African National Congress headquarters in Johannesburg to offer thanks for its cooperation and to pick up a few trinkets as souvenirs. The day after our visit, a bomb went off in that building. It was a jarring reminder of the danger we faced. Armed guards were stationed at our hotel, and we were told not to leave the hotel alone after dark. When I went out at dawn for a morning jog in another city, I encountered high barbed-wire fences, snarling dogs, and nasty looks and comments from white locals. It was clear that our team's enthusiasm for universal suffrage in South Africa was not universally shared.

Several times during visits to the polls those three days, I was too moved to stand silently and watch. I was disturbed by the fear in voters' faces at one polling place when a noisy helicopter landed and burly, white Afrikaner men wearing shorts, knee socks, and guns in holsters got out. I walked up to the men, introduced myself as part of the UN elections monitoring team (I had my vest on!), and asked, "Who are you? Are you here to vote?" When they shrugged in reply, I said in my most authoritative voice, "You can't be here unless you are planning to vote, in which case you'll have to go stand in this line." They spoke for a moment among themselves, then boarded their helicopter and left. The relief in the voting queue was palpable.

At another polling place in the northern Transvaal township of Bochum, I walked among the hundreds of people waiting to vote to have a chat. Many had been in line for most of a day; some said they had stayed in line overnight to avoid losing their places. Mothers carried infants on their backs and shielded them from the scorching sun with colorful umbrellas. Many wore their best clothes to show respect for the opportunity to vote that was finally theirs. They were thrilled to be there.[8]

As a United Nations elections observer with poll workers in Bochum Township in what was then Lebowa, Northern Transvaal, South Africa, 1994

"Don't worry, we have plenty of ballots," I assured one older woman. "It won't be much longer now."

She reassured me in turn: "I've waited eighty years to vote. Another few hours won't matter."

The balloting was extremely slow, in part because so many of the new voters were illiterate. They needed help marking their ballots, which were printed with photos as well as the names of the candidates. I heard, "I want to vote for the old man . . . the one who was in prison . . . the man with the white hair." Those were votes for Nelson Mandela, the African National Congress leader who was elected South Africa's first black president in that election. Election workers were not allowed to touch the completed ballots. But that meant they had to take some elderly voters by the hand and guide their hands to place the ballot into a sealed box. After each ballot was added, election

workers shook the box to make sure the marked paper had gone
through the slot properly. That step slowed the process considerably.

"We take our right to vote and participate too much for granted," I
told a St. Cloud audience a few days after my return. "I wish we could
look at our [electoral] process with the same fervor and reverence . . .
and faith" that South Africans exhibited. I consider those voters democracy's heroes.[9]

• • •

Don't rest on your laurels. That's good advice for states as well as individuals. It's the sentiment that kept me looking for new ways to boost
political participation rates in Minnesota. As the 1991 legislative
session began, I floated a raft of ideas: Automatic voter registration
whenever anyone renews a driver's license or obtains a state ID card.
Allowing voters to cast ballots in places other than their home precinct's polling station, after proving their identity with an electronic
card. The production and distribution of a voter information pam-
phlet or website that's tailored for every precinct in the state, including information about candidates and ballot questions. Outreach to
high school students, including voter registration in high schools for
those turning eighteen before the next election. "No excuses" absentee voting—an idea I had raised without success several years before.
And voting by mail—specifically in the 1992 presidential primary. All
of those ideas faced uphill battles at the legislature. Some were ig-
nored completely; others were set on the shelf for years. But the possibility of conducting a presidential primary entirely by mail intrigued
Minnesotans sufficiently to get a serious look by legislators.[10]

State lawmakers had opened the door ever so slightly to mail-only
elections in Minnesota in that 1987 legislation. All-mail elections had
proven themselves to produce both higher voter participation and
lower administrative costs. The law allowed unregistered voters in
all-mail elections to register by mail as well, using the same process
we had created for absentee voters. Mail ballots are submitted in an
unsigned, "secrecy" envelope accompanied by a certificate signed by
both the voter and a witness, who could be any other registered voter
in the voter's county. Completed ballots can be submitted either by

mail or by personal delivery to county auditors' offices before 8 PM on Election Day.[11]

I argued that the 1992 presidential primary presented a fine opportunity for Minnesotans to test the use of mail balloting in a statewide election. Its results were to be binding on Independent-Republicans as they selected national convention delegates, but under the rules agreed to with the Democratic National Committee, the primary's outcome would not be binding on the DFL. It would be the first presidential primary for the state since 1956, revived after years of relying exclusively on low-turnout precinct caucuses to start the process of national delegate selection. I was convinced that balloting by mail would significantly boost voter participation—and in my book, that was what mattered most. A typical primary election in Minnesota in those years drew about 35 percent of eligible voters to the polls. Experience with mail elections in Minnesota and elsewhere suggested that with that voting method, turnout might double. There was another advantage too: presidential primaries are elections in which no state candidates are on the ballot. Legislators could try mail elections without their own skin in the game. I went so far as to propose a funding source to cover the postage costs, which would be borne by state government, not the local governments that ordinarily cover most election expenses. I suggested that the state increase lobbyists' annual registration fees from $100 to $125 per client.[12]

That funding suggestion met with predictable resistance, and contributed to the legislature's inaction on the vote-by-mail primary bill in 1991. So did a competing desire on the part of some insiders in both major parties. They wanted to kill the presidential primary entirely, out of fear that it would further reduce participation in the parties' precinct caucuses, where future volunteers, donors, and candidates are identified and recruited. But the possibility of an all-mail primary was still alive at the January start of the 1992 session. I told lawmakers that if they acted by mid-January and supplied my office with adequate funding, Minnesota could have the nation's first all-mail primary on April 7—and it likely could generate turnout high enough to attract national notice and give Minnesota voters the clout they had long lacked in presidential nomination contests. The *Star Tribune* editorial board got behind the idea, arguing that "ahead of all other legislative responsibilities comes the need to ensure the continued functioning of representative democracy." But the legislature balked, and instead sent Governor Arne Carlson a bill to cancel the 1992 primary. Carlson promptly vetoed that bill. The 1992 primary election, conducted in the conventional fashion, went forward—and attracted a pitiful ten percent of eligible voters to the polls. The exercise was so unpopular with the two parties that they made Minnesota's presidential primary disappear for another twenty-eight years.[13]

• • •

Arne Carlson vetoed 178 full or partial bills during eight years in office, far more than any other governor in state history. He wielded his veto pen with such relish that one can fairly conclude that it was his favorite instrument of gubernatorial power. That adds irony to the fact that during his first year in office, 1991, he made a timing error that nullified fourteen vetoes. Among them was his attempt to strike down a redistricting bill that Republicans said would give DFLers an advantage in congressional and legislative elections for the next decade. It was an embarrassing and politically damaging mistake by the new governor—one in which my office played a small role.[14]

When Tom Durand arrived to open our office's front door at about 8 AM on June 7, he was startled to find a batch of veto messages from the governor's office on the floor in front of the door. Tom knew that was a highly irregular way to submit veto messages to our office for official filing. He immediately counted the days. The Minnesota Constitution specifies that a governor has three days (Sundays excluded) to act on a bill presented to him during a legislative session. While the 1991–92 session had begun its official recess on May 20, the session had not ended. The three-day rule still applied. Several of the bills in question had been presented to the governor on May 31, a Friday. The three-day rule meant that the most recent of vetoes should have been delivered to either the secretary of the state Senate or the chief clerk of the House on June 4, and to us very soon thereafter. They were late. Tom consulted with me, and at my direction, he called the attorney general's office.[15]

A quick review found that in all, fourteen bills that Carlson attempted to veto in the days after the legislature's recess had missed the three-day deadline. That stunning news was splashed across the *Star Tribune*'s front page on June 8, including Carlson's accusations that a cabal of DFLers was falsely maligning him. His press secretary, Tim Droogsma, said that my office had advised the governor's office that veto messages had only to be signed within three days, not returned to the affected bills' chamber of origin. That was not true; in fact, Carlson's office had spurned offers of guidance about veto procedures earlier that year from both my office and that of the attorney general. In August, Ramsey County district judge Joanne M. Smith sided with me. I was grateful that her findings of fact included this: "Secretary of State Growe has herself taken no action either to cause such bills to become law or to prevent them from becoming law."

After Smith's order was filed, Carlson dropped his effort to get the courts to uphold his veto. Other Republicans weren't through asking the courts to draw legislative and congressional district maps that they deemed more favorable to their party. Two more years of legal back-and-forth ensued before maps were approved that were only slightly different from the ones Carlson attempted to veto in 1991. The lengthy litigation upheld my position that state courts, not federal ones, have jurisdiction to draw new district lines if the legislature and governor fail to act. The 1990–92 redistricting was the only occasion since the 1960s in which Minnesota's legislators, rather than judges, drew the new political maps required in the wake of each decennial US census. In every other decade, divided state government led to political impasses that have tossed redistricting to the judiciary.[16]

In my view, political mapmaking by nonpartisan judges, not partisan legislators, has been a plus for good governance. Minnesota has been spared from the gerrymandering that in other states has created too many "safe" districts, which in turn has empowered extremists within both major parties while discouraging turnout and political participation among more moderate voters. In fact, I've been saying for some time that I believe the judicial branch should take over redistricting on a permanent basis. I was part of a 2008 blue-ribbon task force convened by former vice president Walter Mondale and former governor Arne Carlson that recommended that the legislature give the task to a commission of retired judges. As I had seen many times before, legislators are extremely reluctant to surrender power to anyone else. Despite our task force's distinguished pedigree, its recommendations have not been adopted. But as another redistricting cycle is about to begin in the state, I'm hoping that report will be remembered and its ideas revived.[17]

• • •

The cold shoulder legislators were giving my ideas for election innovation left me determined to do more with my own authority—and my office's limited budget—to encourage citizen participation in politics and government. In 1992, I launched First Vote, an effort to educate and register first-time voters while they were still in high school. It was a joint project of my office, the state Department of Education, the League of Women Voters, and several civic-minded corporations. That same year, I enlisted the help of a half dozen businesses in making voter registration forms available at their retail outlets. It was a coup when the ubiquitous fast-food purveyor McDonald's agreed to supply their patrons with registration forms upon request—and also when Cub Foods grocery stores printed a voting reminder on their grocery bags. A spokesperson for the McDonald's corporate decision makers told the *Star Tribune* that the chance to reach young voters convinced them to work with us. That corporate push led to a 50 percent increase in new voter registrations in September and October 1992, compared with the same months four years earlier.[18]

For that year's September primary, I also introduced something small that has become a big hit with Minnesota voters. I came back from a National Association of Secretaries of State meeting with an idea: Why not give voters an "I Voted" sticker they could take with them and wear after voting? Joe got busy and crafted a red-and-white round sticker that simply read "I Voted." The stickers were in big demand right from the start. We ordered several million of them for distribution on November 3 and hoped we would need all of them.

But a major snowstorm socked Minnesota on Election Day. That, plus the fact that no state constitutional office or US Senate seat was on the 1992 ballot, can be blamed for knocking Minnesota into second place among the states in turnout, with a 73.9 percent showing. Given the weather, I considered that a satisfying result, though it stung a little that the nation's turnout leader that year was Minnesota's neighbor and Big Ten football rival, Wisconsin.[19]

The next election would be different, I assured anyone who asked about that drop in national turnout rankings. Minnesota's governorship and an open US Senate seat were on the 1994 ballot. (Dave Durenberger announced on September 16, 1993, that he would not seek reelection.) Both contests would be the kind that pull Minnesotans to the polls, I said.

That prediction began to look shaky early in the 1994 political year. Turnout at the March 1 precinct caucuses was low—fewer than thirty thousand in each party, or less than one percent of the party's vote in the most recent statewide election. Precinct caucuses never draw as many participants as primary elections do. But their defenders—which included me—like the grassroots engagement in democracy that caucuses encourage. Caucuses bring like-minded neighbors together one night every two years for conversations about both candidates and issues. Despite their reputation as insular and complicated, both parties' caucuses in Minnesota are typically welcoming and low-key. Those who participate often go on to volunteer for campaigns, serve as convention delegates, donate money, and run for office themselves. What's more, candidates who opt to seek party endorsement usually can do so on a smaller budget than is required for successful candidates who skip caucuses and conventions and go directly to the primary ballot. That, too, makes for a more inclusive democracy.[20]

But Minnesota's 1994 experience also illustrates what can result when precinct caucus turnout is low. A disproportionate share of the Minnesotans who bothered to show up at caucuses that March were hard-core partisans whose thinking about government put them to the left of many in the DFL and to the right of many Independent-Republican voters. The process those caucuses launched concluded at state conventions a few months later. Both parties endorsed candidates for governor who lacked broad appeal.

Independent-Republicans stunned many observers by rejecting Arne Carlson, the popular incumbent governor of their own party, in favor of former, three-term state representative Allen Quist, an outspoken opponent of legal abortion and LGBTQ rights. Quist easily topped Carlson at the convention, winning 69 percent of delegates' votes on the first and only ballot. Carlson wore Quist's accusation that he was a "moderate Republican" as a badge of honor into the September 13 primary, and used it to good effect as he outpolled Quist by nearly two to one.[21]

DFLers in 1994 endorsed as their gubernatorial candidate state senator John Marty, a thirty-eight-year-old champion of ethics in government who ranked among the most liberal members of the legislature. Concern about his electability brought him two formidable primary opponents, Minneapolis police chief Tony Bouza and former state commerce commissioner Mike Hatch. Hatch came within 5,353 votes of denying Marty the nomination. That narrow primary win foretold Marty's fate in the general election. Carlson cruised to victory, winning 63 percent of the vote.

• • •

Well before the 1994 Election Day, I started talking about ways that Minnesota's candidate selection process could be changed to encourage more citizen participation—and in so doing, bolster something that's fundamental to democracy: majority rule. When too few people select candidates, the democratic legitimacy of government is eroded. I had come to the secretary of state's office twenty years earlier intent on shoring up turnout in elections. Increasingly, I saw that turnout at precinct caucuses also needed shoring up, and that the secretary of state could play a role in making that happen. I had been gathering ideas from other states as part of the National Commission for the Renewal of American Democracy, founded by the National Association of Secretaries of State in 1992. Soon after the 1994 precinct caucuses, I shared my thinking with the *Star Tribune*'s editorial board. The result was a lengthy editorial published on March 13 that included some of my ideas:

- Increase the political stakes in caucus participation by making party endorsement the easiest path to the primary election ballot. Increase the petition-signature requirement for unendorsed candidates to a significant number from a variety of locations. In a statewide race, for example, the requirement could be five thousand signatures from each of the state's eight congressional districts.
- Require parties to endorse and advance to the primary ballot any candidate who achieves more than minimal support at a party-endorsing convention. Two other states used that method. In Colorado, any candidate with the votes of more than 30 percent of a convention's delegates automatically was placed on the primary ballot. In Connecticut, the threshold was 15 percent.
- Move the primary election to the third week in June. That would shorten the intraparty phase of the candidate selection process, which now lasts until mid-August. It would also compel candidates to devote time and money earlier to the whole electorate rather than to only a few thousand convention delegates. That would get citizens into the political action sooner.
- Make caucuses more visible and newcomer-friendly, starting with scheduling them during daytime hours on a weekend. Minnesota's traditional Tuesday, cold-winter's-night caucus time excludes too many people. I fancied the notion of creating a new holiday, Minnesota Democracy Day, that could include party-sponsored issue forums, internet-enabled video conferencing with candidates, and potluck meals, as well as the customary meetings. In my imaginings, the day would culminate with the announcement of the results of straw polls conducted earlier in the day—and, in presidential years, the results of a mail ballot–only, presidential primary election.[22]

The positive reception that editorial received helped propel my next step. During the summer of 1994, I recruited and convened an eighteen-member, bipartisan Growe Commission on Electoral Reform. Its task: to develop recommendations for increasing participation in

Minnesota's candidate endorsement and nomination process. It was truly a blue-ribbon commission. Among its members were a former IR state chair and a former DFL state chair, two IR and two DFL legislators, two University of Minnesota professors, and the leaders of groups including the League of Women Voters, the Jefferson Center, Common Cause, the Humphrey Forum, and the Minnesota Study Circles Network.[23]

My timing raised a few eyebrows. The 1994 campaign was in full swing as the commission began its work that September—and that campaign included me. I was on the ballot that year seeking a sixth term. My IR opponent, Richard Kimbler, was a self-employed insurance businessman from Ramsey who had previously made a short-lived run for governor. He touted a number of bad ideas, including making the secretary of state an appointive rather than elective office and ending the office's efforts to make the voting process more convenient. A story about him in the *Brainerd Daily Dispatch* featured a damning headline: "Kimbler: Not Everyone Needs to Vote." Those were flawed notions that I needed to refute. I couldn't spend all fall in St. Paul. With Joe Mansky staffing the commission and drafting its final report, I knew its work was in good hands. I considered it important for the commission to act soon after both parties had seen the consequences of low-turnout precinct caucuses. I'd given the seventeen commission members a tight deadline. My aim was to bring their recommendations to the 1995 legislature in January.[24]

With my sixth term secure—I won reelection by more than a half million votes—and with the commission's work completed shortly before the new year, I prepared for an uphill battle at the legislature. The commission did excellent work. Its recommendations to the legislature were direct and specific. The commission adopted most of them unanimously; those that were not were so noted in the final report. The advice:

- Conduct precinct caucuses during daytime hours on a weekend in April.
- Move the state primary election from the second week in September to the first or second week in August.

- Conduct presidential primaries by mail, with ballots returned and counted on the same day as precinct caucuses.
- Give a place on the state primary ballot to major-party candidates for state and federal offices who receive at least 20 percent of the vote on any ballot at a party-endorsing convention, or who submit a petition signed by eligible voters equal to 10 percent of the persons voting for nomination to that office in the last state primary.
- Identify party-endorsed candidates on primary ballots.
- Rename the primary the "party nomination election."
- Permit corporations to make tax-deductible contributions to the secretary of state to promote voter participation in both precinct caucuses and elections on a nonpartisan basis.
- Require and provide funding for the secretary of state to make voter information available to the public via a toll-free telephone line, to produce and make available to the public a video explaining how to participate in the precinct caucuses, and to prepare and distribute to each household in the state a voter's guide prior to the precinct caucuses, the state primary election, and the state general election.

One might think that the voter-education elements in that last recommendation would be easily approved. But in 1994 Governor Arne Carlson demonstrated otherwise when he vetoed funding for the toll-free voter-information hotline. He also nixed a bill that would have authorized my office to allow youth under the age of eighteen to vote in mock elections on primary and general Election Days. That latter veto stung, in part because Carlson's veto letter claimed that the Kids Vote program I proposed "could easily become a partisan tool rather than an educational aid." The *Star Tribune* called those accusatory words "ungracious," especially given my unbiased handling of the 1990 gubernatorial election that put him in office. They were indeed ungracious—and they were also a fresh reminder, as if I needed one, that *any* election law revision is a tough sell among politicians who think themselves well served by the status quo.[25]

Still, I thought that the commission's ideas were so sensible, and the case for change was so strong, that they had a chance at the DFL-controlled 1995 legislature. The editorial pages of both the Minneapolis and St. Paul newspapers backed them. So did the state Senate, which sent a strong bill to the House. But there the bill stalled, then died. The motives of the House DFL leaders who killed the bill were many and varied, but one particularly disappointed me. As a *Star Tribune* postmortem editorial put it, "Some wanted to aid their special-interest friends—particularly the anti-abortion lobby—who fare better in both parties when participation is low." There's a word for that thinking: undemocratic. In fact, that single word was the editorial's headline.[26]

● ● ●

I kept talking about the importance of voting and attending caucuses. I kept promoting ideas like no-excuses absentee voting, conducting primaries by mail, and a toll-free hotline for voting information. I kept traveling the state to keep county auditors up to speed about election laws and to provide the tools needed to train thirty thousand election judges every two years. I welcomed the arrival of the internet and worked with my wonderful staff to take advantage of that tool. I considered myself very lucky to work with the finest secretary of state's staff in the country. My deputy secretary, Elaine Voss, my administrator, Rich Pietz, and I were so close that we could finish each other's sentences. The three of us had a rule: if one of us said we were having a bad day, no one else among the three of us could have a bad day that day. We insisted on keeping the office environment positive.

Nevertheless, the legislature's rejection of the Growe Commission report was a turning point in my service as secretary of state. That report was the culmination of more than twenty years of work to keep democracy strong in Minnesota, and it had not been well received where it counted, among the state's lawmakers. That was a bitter pill, especially since the rejection came at the hands of the leaders of the DFL House majority. Legislators did not seem to share my concern about declining voter participation in the state and in the nation as a whole. Minnesota's election turnout had slipped to sixth among the states in 1994, and was back up to second in 1996—but that year's

In office, 1996. Larry Marcus

turnout, 65 percent, was the lowest for any presidential election since the state began keeping records in 1950.[27]

On September 11, 1997, I announced that I would not seek a seventh term in 1998. I had two young granddaughters then and another one on the way. I wanted to spend time with them, I explained. The news caught some Minnesotans by surprise—or so said Tony Sutton, the executive director of the newly renamed Minnesota Republican Party. (The "Independent" brand had fallen out of fashion with a state party that now seemed fully in sync with its national counterpart, and was dropped in 1995.) "Wow—we don't even have anyone in the wings," Sutton told a *Star Tribune* reporter. "She was so popular it was hard to recruit candidates against her."[28]

I was glad that the recaps of my career that accompanied news of my retirement mentioned my efforts to encourage and advise other women seeking elective office. I had been making a point to do that since 1973. I cheered as the number of women in the 201-member Minnesota Legislature grew from six when I served in the state House to sixty-three in 1997.

But there it stalled. In 2019, sixty-four women occupied legislative seats. In 1994, another DFL woman—Ann Wynia, a brilliant college professor, former House majority leader, and former state human services commissioner—ran for the US Senate seat that Durenberger had occupied for sixteen years. She came closer to winning than I had against Boschwitz ten years earlier. But it hurt to watch highly qualified and gifted Ann lose to Rod Grams, an archconservative Republican whose professional background was as a news reader on the Twin Cities' Fox TV affiliate. Grams became the Republican nominee that year by defeating Carlson's lieutenant governor, Joanell Dyrstad, in that party's primary. Minnesota's Republicans did not nominate a woman for the US Senate until choosing state senator Karin Housley to run against US senator Tina Smith in 2018. Smith won that election with a margin of more than 10 percentage points.

It's a joy to see two exceptional DFL women, Smith and Amy Klobuchar, representing Minnesota in the Senate, and to note that DFL women hold three of Minnesota's eight US House seats—Angie

Craig in the Second District, Betty McCollum in the Fourth, and Ilhan Omar in the Fifth. But it's frustrating to report that Minnesota
has yet to elect a female governor.

I didn't let my lame-duck status—or my election-observer trip to
Azerbaijan that fall—relax my office's get-out-the-vote effort in 1998.
My voice was on public-service radio announcements aired all over
the state, urging people to vote. I did my customary calculations to
project turnout, this time factoring in the growing excitement about
a three-way contest for governor. A third-party candidate, former
professional wrestler and talk-radio host Jesse Ventura, was rapidly
climbing in the polls against Republican Norm Coleman, a former
St. Paul mayor, and DFLer Hubert H. "Skip" Humphrey III, the state's
attorney general since 1983. I said turnout would be high—and it was.
Minnesota was back on top among the states in voter participation
in 1998, and Ventura became the state's first third-party governor in
sixty years. Analysts noted that Election Day registration was crucial to Ventura's victory. In Anoka County, for example, more than
twenty-two thousand voters registered on Election Day, producing
turnout rivaling that in a presidential election year. Ventura, whose
statewide winning margin was just 37 percent, carried Anoka County
with 51 percent of the vote.[29]

Ventura famously said as he celebrated his victory that Minnesota
voters had "shocked the world" by electing him. It was indeed a jolt
to the two major parties. But it also demonstrated something enduring about Minnesota elections that I had sought to safeguard and
promote through twenty-four years as secretary of state. Minnesota's
electoral system is not the plaything of political insiders. It belongs
to the people—a people who through many years have prized their
political independence. Elections in Minnesota are open and adapt-
able enough to allow a challenger to party insiders to rise up and
win. They are also held in such respect that none of the losers in 1998
challenged the legitimacy of Ventura's win or sought to end Election
Day registration in its wake. Even Minnesotans who had not voted
for Ventura felt pride in a system that made his win possible. As I left
office, so did I.

10

How to Keep the State That Votes

It has been more than twenty years since I had any personal responsibility for the conduct of Minnesota's elections. But I'm more convinced today than I was as secretary of state that Minnesotans owe much to their willingness to vote and their ability to do so with little impediment. I see high voter turnout as a major factor in Minnesota's success story. It has been crucial to giving state and local government both the legitimacy and the limits it needs to function well.

Minnesotans are rightfully proud of the state they've built. Although they know there are still problems to solve—including a damaging racial divide to bridge—Minnesotans take pride in knowing that for the past five presidential elections, their state's voter turnout led the nation. I hope they see a connection between high voter turnout and the features of Minnesota life that they enjoy. I believe the link is very strong.

The chief challenges that remain in election administration today are much the same as they were during my tenure in office: how can Minnesota increase voter participation in low-income neighborhoods and among people of color? Those populations have fewer of the resources that regular voting requires: information, transportation, child care, and the confidence built on solid evidence that their votes matter.

Yet the Somali American community in Minneapolis has shown what's possible. Since the 1990s, Minnesota has been a prime US destination for people fleeing civil war in Somalia; the 2017 American Community Survey put the state's Somali American population at more than fifty-two thousand. Candidates from that community began filing for local and state offices in 2010, when the late Hussein Samatar was the first Somali American to win a seat on the Minneapolis school board. In short order he was followed by the first Somali American member of the Minneapolis City Council, Abdi Warsame. With those candidacies came a surge in voter participation, which in turn contributed to the election of US representative Ilhan Omar from the state's Fifth Congressional District.[1]

After spending many years wrestling with election issues, I watch today's election developments with both concern and determination. Trends elsewhere in the nation are reaching Minnesota with the potential to erode voter participation. Minnesotans should take note of those trends with a wary eye. They have something precious to protect.

To be sure, other people have different perspectives and priorities. My immediate successor in the secretary of state's office was Mary Kiffmeyer, a Republican who served two terms and is now a state senator and the point person for her Republican majority caucus on election issues. As secretary of state, she focused her energies on preventing voter fraud—despite the absence of evidence that Minnesota elections produced more than a handful of episodes of ineligible people casting ballots. And she did not consider Election Day registration to be key to Minnesota's consistently high turnout; in testimony before a congressional committee, she said that "It's not the ultimate predictor at all."[2]

The facts say otherwise. Research has consistently shown that Election Day registration increases turnout, with gains in the range of 3 to 7 percentage points. It does so more reliably than a number of other voting innovations, including early voting. The National Conference of State Legislatures reports that states with Election Day registration consistently outperform other states in turnout. Introduced in 1973–74 in Minnesota, Maine, and Wisconsin, it's now available in twenty states; one more, New Mexico, approved it in 2019 for phased implementation over the next several years. I fully concur with Minnesota's secretary of state in 2020, DFLer Steve Simon. When he describes Minnesota's reputation for clean and effective democracy, he calls Election Day registration "the jewel in our crown."[3]

But resistance to Election Day registration was spreading among Republicans in the early 2000s. Those years saw a widening of the nation's partisan divide over many issues. Disagreements over immigration, climate change, gun control, same-sex marriage, and tax policy hardened into orthodoxy in both parties. That led to gridlock in both Congress and any state with divided government, which Minnesota has experienced for twenty-eight of the thirty years between 1990 and 2020. It's no coincidence that twice during that period, in 2005 and 2011, an inability to find bipartisan compromise on the Minnesota state budget led to prolonged partial shutdowns of state government—black eyes for the state *Time* magazine had once dubbed "the state that works."[4]

At the same time, a sharp difference in the two parties' positions on voting and democracy itself emerged. Republicans in Minnesota and around the country noticed in the post-Reagan years that their candidates tended to fare better in low-turnout elections. They saw that in much of the country, nonvoters were disproportionately those with below-average incomes, people of color, and young adults—people Republicans believed favored Democratic candidates. Republicans increasingly equated a push for higher turnout with efforts to elect more Democrats. They pushed back—not by competing more vigorously, but by seeking to bar some would-be voters from the polls. While these tactics are often advanced in the name of fraud prevention, they are more accurately described as vote suppression. Wittingly or not, they are taking the nation in the direction of minority rule.[5]

Through the early 2000s, Republican officeholders told Minnesotans that fraud was a problem in our elections. Despite the absence of evidence to back those claims, many Minnesotans were inclined to believe them and to see a photo ID requirement as a reasonable antifraud measure. In 2012, the Republican-controlled legislature sent to the state's voters a proposed constitutional amendment that would have required voters to show a government-issued photo-identification card before receiving a ballot. (The legislature's GOP majorities were prevented from imposing the photo ID requirement by state statute because any such bill faced a sure veto by DFL governor Mark Dayton. In Minnesota, constitutional amendments do not require a governor's signature to go to the ballot.) All that year, polls showed that a majority of Minnesotans favored the photo ID requirement.[6]

Fortunately, a strong campaign against the amendment was waged by Our Vote Our Future, a coalition whose eighty-eight member organizations included the League of Women Voters, the state AFL-CIO, AARP, the Minnesota Farmers Union, and a number of civil rights groups. The coalition pointed out that a 2006 study by the Brennan Center for Justice at New York University Law School found that 11 percent of America's eligible voters lack ready access to a photo ID of the type the proposed amendment would require. That segment of the US population is disproportionately poor, elderly, and people of color, some of whom were born in the rural South at a time when the birth certificates required for the issuance of photo ID cards were often not filed for at-home births. The same study found that an additional ten percent of Americans at any given time carry a photo ID card with an address that is not current and thus would be invalid at the polls.[7]

Joe Mansky was an outspoken opponent of the proposed photo ID amendment. Joe left the secretary of state's office not long after I did to become elections manager for Ramsey County, Minnesota's second-largest county and home to the state capitol. That role allowed him to continue to function as the state's leading authority on best practices in election administration. As he told the state Senate Finance Committee on March 1, 2012, the proposed requirement of a government-issued photo ID would be burdensome to students at Minnesota's many private colleges, whose student ID cards are not issued by a government entity. He also noted that possession of a valid driver's license is no assurance of eligibility to vote. Felons whose voting rights have not yet been restored often have valid licenses. The same applies to legal immigrants who are not US citizens.[8]

Traditionally, Minnesotans have insisted on fairness in matters of law and democracy. Information like that turned the tide. So did criticism of the amendment by former vice president Walter Mondale, former governor Arne Carlson, incumbent governor Dayton, and me. In the days before the election, highly effective TV ads featuring Carlson and Dayton pointed out the disenfranchisement that the amendment could cause.

The amendment was defeated with a solid 52–46 percent vote. Minnesota was the first state to reject a photo ID requirement when it was presented to voters at the ballot box. Notably, the amendment failed in forty-four of the state's eighty nonmetro counties, places that had been trending Republican in previous elections. Those rural counties have a larger share of elderly voters than metro counties do. I like to think those voters recognized the burden a photo ID requirement would have placed on seniors who no longer maintain valid driver's licenses.[9]

Those who want to make voting more difficult for some segments of the population have not given up on the photo ID tactic. North Dakota is the only state that does not require voter registration. In 2018, its Republican-controlled legislature passed a law requiring voters to show an ID with a current street address in order to receive a ballot. That requirement was particularly burdensome to an estimated five thousand Indigenous North Dakotans who live on reservations, receive their mail at post office boxes, and do not have street addresses. Tribal ID cards were not acceptable for voting purposes under the new law. Lawsuits were filed to attempt to block the new requirement, to no avail. The Native American Rights Fund got busy before the election and provided more than two thousand people with the documentation they needed to vote. But those efforts still left a substantial number of people disenfranchised.[10]

• • •

Photo ID requirements are not the only trick in the vote-suppression book. Purging voters from registration rolls—something every state does to some degree to keep lists up to date—has been done aggressively in a number of states to disqualify large numbers from voting. It was a tactic that Florida's Republican secretary of state Katherine Harris used in that state in the run-up to the 2000 presidential election. Florida's registration purges are credited with—or blamed for—helping to elect George W. Bush as president. Since then, names have been purged in some states for as little as failing to vote in two consecutive elections, or for not responding to a mailed postcard within a limited period of time. This tactic is particularly prevalent in the South, a 2018 Brennan Center study found. Only one state in the old Confederacy, North Carolina, offers Election Day registration, and then only during early voting. Almost four million more names were removed from registration rolls between 2014 and 2016 than between 2006 and 2008, the study reported. That's a 33 percent increase, compared with a population increase of 6 percent and an increase in registered voters of 18 percent during the same period.[11]

An aggressive voter registration purge in the state of Georgia caught national attention because of the role it likely played in the 2018 defeat of a very impressive Democratic candidate for governor, former Georgia House minority leader Stacey Abrams. Her Republican opponent and the contest's winner, Brian Kemp, was the Georgia secretary of state. He had overseen the removal of 750,000 more registrations between the 2012 and 2016 elections than had been removed between 2008 and 2012. Kemp won by just under fifty-five thousand votes in an election that produced multiple complaints about irregularities. For example: less than a month before the election, it was reported that Kemp was refusing to process some fifty-three thousand voter registration applications, 80 percent of them from black voters, because they did not exactly match names on file elsewhere in state government records. Days before the November 6 election, a federal judge ordered Kemp to process the registration applications of an additional three thousand voters who had recently become US citizens but whose citizenship status had not been updated by Kemp's office.[12]

To her credit, Stacey Abrams has become a national crusader for voting rights in the year since her defeat. She's the founder of Fair Fight, a new nonprofit organization that promotes voter education and participation, advocates for election reform, and conducts targeted voter registration drives. I'm impressed with Abrams and her organization, and I consider her an important leader in the struggle to give America a more inclusive democracy.[13]

Sadly, overly aggressive voter purges have not stopped. Georgia was at it again in 2019. That state's new secretary of state released a list in October 2019 of 313,000 voters whose registrations are at risk of deletion. A purge has also begun in Wisconsin—a sorry development in a state that joined Minnesota in early enactment of Election Day registration in the 1970s. A Wisconsin judge ruled on December 13, 2019, that 234,000 names should be dropped from voter registration rolls because those voters had failed to respond to postcards sent to the addresses associated with their registrations. Since Wisconsin voters can register at the polls, purging their names from preregistration lists won't technically prevent them from voting. But the time and the proof-of-residency requirements associated with an unexpected discovery that one must register anew might well send some discouraged would-be voters out the door before they cast ballots—and those especially inconvenienced are likely to be people who work in low-wage jobs. For them, time away from work typically means the loss of essential income.[14]

Minnesota has avoided aggressive voter purges with a system that carefully defends the system's integrity. The secretary of state's office mails postcards to newly registered voters and those who register a change of name or address. Names and addresses of those returned as undeliverable are noted as "challenged" in Minnesota's voter registration files. That does not mean they are ineligible to vote. Rather, it means their eligibility is in question. When they arrive at their polling places, challenged voters must satisfy election judges with information about their residency before they can vote. That's Minnesota's way of providing a voter with due process before eligibility is denied. Often, the matter is easily resolved. Such cases can involve people who recently moved, took a new name because of marriage or divorce, or were temporarily not receiving mail because of a trip, hospitalization, or nursing-home stay. People who move frequently—generally, those with low incomes and college students—are disproportionately noted as "challenged."

A lawsuit brought in 2017 by the Minnesota Voters Alliance, a litigious conservative group that bills itself as "election integrity watchdogs," seemed intended to discourage voting by anyone on Minnesota's "challenged" list. The suit sought the public release of the names and addresses of challenged voters. Secretary of State Steve Simon argued that such information is rightfully private. He said he feared the Voters Alliance intended to contact those people with intimidating messages suggesting they had voted illegally and are possibly subject to felony charges. (Illegal voting in Minnesota carries stiff penalties.) Fortunately, in a 5–2 decision, the Minnesota Supreme Court sided with Simon in April 2020. But the Voters Alliance made clear that it considers the court ruling a mere "setback," and plans to press its argument in the future at the Minnesota Legislature.[15]

Private attempts to intimidate voters, no matter their status, should not happen. Violations of state election laws are crimes that ought to be treated as any other. In this country, the state must prove that someone has committed a crime before that person is sanctioned. Those who challenge voters' eligibility appear to have a different concept. They evidently think some people should be required to prove that they are eligible before they can exercise their constitutional right. That's fundamentally wrong. A prospective voter should be assumed innocent of criminal activity unless he or she is proven guilty. It is the *state's* obligation to properly monitor voter registration records and prove from the data available that a would-be voter is ineligible. That's in keeping with my bedrock belief that in America, voting is a right, not a privilege. Minnesota takes the additional step of asking new registrants to confirm their eligibility in writing, under oath and penalty of perjury. Decades of clean, verifiable elections in Minnesota attest to the sufficiency of those measures.

• • •

More vote-suppression mischief is behind the national push for provisional balloting in states with Election Day registration, and this has had implications even in Minnesota. Provisional ballots were invented several decades ago as a remedy for voters with uncertain registration status in states that don't allow voters to register on Election Day. Such a voter who appears at the polls is issued a provisional ballot, which is set aside and not counted unless the voter provides proof of his or her eligibility to vote within a brief window of time after Election Day. That has meant that many provisional ballots are never counted. In 2014, according to the National Conference of State Legislatures, 19.2 percent of provisional ballots cast nationally were never included in final vote totals.[16]

A state with Election Day registration has no need for provisional ballots. That was my successful argument to Congress in 1993, when it exempted states with Election Day registration from a requirement that provisional ballots be made available to voters with uncertain registration status. But when Republicans tried to impose a photo ID requirement in 2012 in Minnesota, they also tried to require that anyone who registers on Election Day must be given a provisional ballot, not a regular one. Had the photo ID amendment become law, the same would go for a long-registered voter who lost or never had a government-issued photo ID card. His or her ballot would be set aside and not counted until election officials could certify the accuracy of the identification information supplied by the new registrant. If even a minor discrepancy was found when comparing new registrations with existing records—a misspelled name, a missing hyphen, the number 5 mistaken for the number 8—the ballot would be rejected. The cost of this additional exercise would be borne by local jurisdictions (in other words, by payers of property taxes) and would total an estimated $15 million statewide in a high-volume election, according to then–secretary of state Mark Ritchie, who served from 2007 to 2015. That cost was among the arguments Ritchie made as he vigorously protested the photo ID/provisional-ballot proposal and helped defeat it.[17]

Ritchie's successor, Steve Simon, warns that Minnesota opponents of same-day registration have not given up on the provisional-ballot idea. They've also begun a push for issuing provisional ballots to any voter whose preregistration has been challenged—the same group whose data is sought by the Voters Alliance lawsuit. The proposal is to provide such voters with provisional ballots and require that they prove their residency within a few days' time in order for their ballots to be counted. They would be required to appear on short notice at their county auditor's office—no short trip in Minnesota's sprawling northern counties—and prove their residency and eligibility for their ballots to be counted. All that effort would be to vote in an election for which they already know the outcome. It's likely that, unless the election is exceedingly close, only the most dedicated voters would make that trip. As a result, more would-be voters would be denied their right to help govern this country and left to believe that their votes don't matter. Provisional balloting is a bad idea that Minnesotans should reject.

• • •

Fortunately, those who want to keep democracy strong by keeping election turnout high can do more than play defense. Several ideas for reducing barriers to the polls are showing their worth in other states.

The most promising new development is automatic voter registration, something I first proposed in 1991. It might be called motor voter 2.0 because it represents a twenty-first-century update of Minnesota's 1987 requirement that voter registration forms be offered to people as they register their vehicles, pay their license tabs, buy hunting and fishing licenses, or transact other business with the state. The difference is that instead of inviting citizens to opt in to voter registration in such settings, they would be automatically registered unless they opt out. The names, addresses, and other requisite information about those who don't opt out would then be sent electronically to election administrators. If a change of address is involved, that update could happen without paper changing hands or anyone making a trip to a county auditor's office.

Automatic voter registration became more feasible within the last decade when most state governments finally developed electronic databases that could be readily shared among agencies. Oregon became the first state to implement it in 2016. (Minnesota could have been the first, if not for Republican governor Tim Pawlenty's veto of the 2009 omnibus elections bill that Republicans in the legislature opposed—in part, I suspect, because it would have made voter registration easier.) In states that have put automatic voter registration in place, the results have been impressive. Oregon's voter registration rates at motor vehicle registration offices quadrupled after the change. Vermont, another early adopter, saw a 62 percent increase in voter registration rates in the first six months of 2017 compared with the same period in 2016.[18]

The idea has caught on rapidly. As of January 2020, sixteen states plus the District of Columbia have automatic registration. I hope that by the time you read this, Minnesota will have joined them. The benefits are considerable. For voters, automatic registrations before Election Day will mean fewer worries, hassles, and unpleasant registration-related surprises at the polls. Many more voters will arrive at the polls to find that they are already registered. In fact, Steve Simon believes the demand for Election Day registration will drop by as much as 80 percent in Minnesota, from 350,000 new registrants on a typical Election Day to something closer to 70,000. For election administrators, a constant stream of updates between their offices and those of other government agencies will mean voter rolls that are more accurate and up-to-date. Electronic data transmission is inexpensive and it avoids human error in the processing of handwritten paper documents. It would also allow voters to check the accuracy of their registration and make any needed corrections before going to the polls, using a secure, online portal.[19]

What's the argument against it? Steve Simon tells me that critics of automatic voter registration say it's too easy. To that, I say: Finally! Voter registration is a nineteenth-century practice concocted to make voting difficult for people on the margins of American life, new immigrant, and former slaves. It's past time that the United States live up to its democratic ideals and make voting easy for all its adult citizens, regardless of age, race, gender—or criminal record.

Denying the vote to convicted felons has an ancient history. Many US states, including Minnesota, wrote some form of criminal disenfranchisement into their constitutions in the nineteenth century. Often, a ban from the polls was imposed for one crime in particular— bribery to alter the outcome of an election. But the practice expanded greatly during the Jim Crow era of the late nineteenth and early twentieth centuries as a way to deny the vote to African Americans who were newly enfranchised by the Fifteenth Amendment to the US Constitution. When combined with criminal justice practices that resulted in the incarceration of a large share of African American men, the disenfranchisement of felons became a particularly effective tool for securing white supremacy.[20]

That history should shame Minnesotans into rethinking this state's restrictions on voting by people who have been convicted of crimes. Minnesota restores voting rights after an offender is completely "off paper"—that is, after he or she has completed not only incarceration but also probation, parole, or supervised release. Twenty other states have similar policies. But Minnesota stands out among them as a state with one of the highest probation rates in the country. In 2019, Minnesota had the nation's fifth-lowest incarceration rate, with 380 of every 100,000 adults behind bars. But it had 2,450 of every 100,000 adults on "community supervision" or probation, with nearly one in five on probation for longer than five years. At every election—despite efforts to inform those on probation about their continued disenfranchisement—some of those who are still "on paper" attempt to cast ballots. Some of them succeed, get caught, and face a felony charge as a result.[21]

That's a terribly harsh outcome for mistakenly doing something society should want to encourage. When a former offender exhibits a desire to rejoin civil society and shoulder its responsibilities, he or she should be congratulated, not slapped with more jail time. For a number of years, advocates have been asking the legislature to restore voting rights after a felon has left prison—or immediately, for those few whose prison sentences are suspended in favor of long periods of probation. They've won some surprising bipartisan support, but have not yet succeeded. In frustration, the Minnesota chapter of the American Civil Liberties Union filed a lawsuit in October 2019 seeking to have Minnesota's restrictions stricken from law on constitutional grounds. One way or another, convicted felons on probation should be allowed to vote.

• • •

One other good idea would encourage more voting by young Minnesotans in the years immediately after they reach age eighteen, the age of eligibility. Steve Simon was finally able to start mock elections in Minnesota high schools in 2015, twenty-one years after my proposal to bring Kids Vote to Minnesota was vetoed by Governor Arne Carlson. It's been very successful. Simon reports that he expected one hundred high schools to participate in the first year, and nearly three hundred signed up. In 2018, 130,000 Minnesota youth voted in the mock election, called Minnesota Students Vote.

The next obvious step is to offer preregistration to high school students ages sixteen and seventeen. Fourteen states plus the District of Columbia offer that option to young people after their sixteenth birthdays; four others do so after age seventeen. Minnesota will allow a young person to register to vote if he or she will be eighteen in time for the next general election. That gets some seventeen-year-olds on the rolls. Minnesota also allows sixteen- and seventeen-year-old high school students to serve as paid election judge trainees. That's a program I initiated in 1991.[22]

But Minnesota is missing an opportunity to get a voter's initial registration done easily, universally, and systematically, in a school setting in which education can be part of the exercise. Preregistrations are automatically converted to full registrations when a voter turns eighteen. Studies have shown that preregistration boosts youth turnout. That boost is needed. Voters between the ages of eighteen and twenty-four are less likely to cast ballots than any other age cohort. Joe Mansky has been pushing for the automatic registration of every high school student in Ramsey County at the time of his or her graduation. That move has seemed particularly appropriate since 2016, when the legislature mandated that every public high school graduate in the state must pass a civics test.[23]

Simon deserves credit for another initiative aimed at increasing young-adult voting. The 2016 and 2018 Minnesota College Ballot Bowl was a voter registration competition among willing campuses. The 2020 Ballot Bowl will go one step further and allow enrolled campuses to compete for achieving the highest voting percentage among their student bodies. The University of Minnesota is demonstrating how easy it is in today's wired world for campuses to promote voting.

Its internal student information website, MyU, includes a link to on-line voter registration and allows students to sign up for text and/or email reminders to vote.[24]

Another idea worth cheering for: set up polling stations on campuses, particularly for early voting. In 2018, during his last year before retiring as elections manager for Ramsey County, Joe Mansky tried that at St. Paul College, and the results were very good. In just seven hours, 271 people voted, forty-one of them for the first time. Joe says he's convinced that every college campus ought to offer an early-voting polling place at least one day before every election.[25]

Joe's experiment with early voting on a community college campus is part of a larger phenomenon that's changing Minnesota voting habits and can be a real plus in efforts to keep turnout high. The switch to "no excuses" absentee voting that I first urged in the mid-1980s finally became state law in 2013. It's been very popular. Prior to the change, about eight percent of Minnesotans cast absentee ballots in typical elections. In 2018, that share was 24 percent, and Simon believes it will keep climbing. Minnesotans can obtain and cast a ballot anytime within forty-six days of the election. It's still an absentee ballot that won't be counted until Election Day, and it can be "clawed back" if a voter appears at the polls and asks to substitute a new ballot for his or her absentee vote. That opportunity distinguishes Minnesota's practice from true early voting, in which one's ballot is cast once and for all when initially filed.

Absentee voting in Minnesota can be done by mail or by visiting one of the growing number of polling stations that local jurisdictions have opened in the days or weeks before the election. Allowing some flexibility for early polling stations invites county auditors and election managers to innovate, as Joe did at St. Paul College. Such experimentation ought to be encouraged, particularly in 2020, as voters seek to cast ballots safely during a global COVID pandemic. (Joe tried another experiment at early voting stations in 2018—issuing pin-on "I Voted" buttons rather than stickers. Buttons can be worn more easily for several days. He reports that the buttons are very popular.)[26]

Minnesotans should be aware that in other states, election watchdogs have seen early voting stations in low-income or predominantly African American neighborhoods closed early or entirely in the run-up to Election Day. The Center for American Progress reports that in Georgia alone, local officials have closed 214 polling locations since 2012, disproportionately affecting poor and minority voters. In 2016, at the urging of that state's Republican Party, North Carolina reduced early voting hours in twenty-three heavily black counties and eliminated Sunday voting in nine counties. As Minnesota expands opportunities to vote before Election Day, it must ensure that those opportunities are widely and uniformly available to all citizens.[27]

A variation on absentee voting that deserves a Minnesota trial soon is to offer "ballot on demand" at polling places, county auditors' offices, or even public libraries. Ballot on demand would allow a Minnesotan to obtain a ballot electronically at a location other than his or her home. For example, a resident of the White Earth Reservation spending the summer in the Twin Cities would be able to go to a polling station in Minneapolis on or before primary Election Day, electronically obtain a ballot from his or her home precinct, and cast a vote securely without having to drive two hundred miles north. That convenience would be especially welcome during summer months, when many Minnesotans work or live away from their fall and winter homes.

• • •

Admittedly, my fixation on voting is uncommonly intense. But as the one hundredth anniversary of the Nineteenth Amendment to the US Constitution is observed in 2020, I'm aware that my thinking is much in keeping with that of Elizabeth Cady Stanton, Susan B. Anthony, Alice Paul, and Carrie Chapman Catt nationally, and Clara Ueland, Mabeth Hurd Paige, and Myrtle Cain in Minnesota. Those suffragists were convinced to their cores that neither individual women nor the nation as a whole could live up to their full potential unless women could vote. They made enormous sacrifices of time and treasure to make it so.

As the first woman elected to a Minnesota statewide office in her own right, I've been called a feminist pioneer. But I stood on the shoulders of giants. And I've tried to befriend and assist the next generations of female officeholders and election administrators in hopes of extending the lineage of women willing to put themselves on the line for democracy.

I'm keenly aware that the struggle for suffrage didn't end one hundred years ago or with women alone. It continued for Native Americans, who were not granted citizenship and suffrage until 1924 and were denied the right to vote in some states for decades after that. It continued for African Americans, particularly in the South, until the 1965 Voting Rights Act became law. Only then did the federal government flex its muscle to enforce the Fifteenth Amendment and end the systematic exclusion of black people from the polls.[28]

It continues still. The US Supreme Court's retreat from the Voting Rights Act in the 2013 case *Shelby County v. Holder* has emboldened states to purge voting rolls and alter polling places in ways that disproportionately discourage voting by African Americans. Georgia's behavior has been egregious, and it is bound to be the subject of litigation for years to come. It deserves strong condemnation. More than that: Congress should consider legislation that would block the worst of the purges of voting rolls, in keeping with the spirit of the original 1965 Voting Rights Act.[29]

But voting rights can also be quite effectively eroded with more subtle means. It can happen when government fails to provide enough polling stations, so that lines at the polls are discouragingly long. It can happen when government fails to keep voting machines operational and sufficient in number. It can happen when social media outlets spew untruths about voting, targeting voters with fear-inducing misinformation or posts calculated to increase cynicism and decrease voting.

It can happen when politicians pay too little heed to cybersecurity, thereby opening electronic registration lists to foreign or domestic hacking. That threat became urgently real in the 2016 presidential election, when, according to the FBI and the US Department of Homeland Security, Russian reconnaissance and hacking attempts were discovered in all fifty states. Unfortunately, some US politicians have been slow to react, or have preferred to play partisan games with the issue. I was dismayed when in 2019 Republicans in the Minnesota Senate delayed the receipt and spending of Minnesota's $6.6 million share of federal funds earmarked for election cybersecurity upgrades. They held up the money for months in hopes of striking a deal with DFLers on other so-called antifraud measures they favor, such as provisional ballots. It was good to hear Steve Simon and Governor Tim Walz publicly condemn Republican intransigence. It was a relief to see that money approved without any strings attached as part of a bipartisan, end-of-session deal. But as technology advances, that $6.6 million must be understood as only a down payment on the sums that will increasingly be needed to keep elections databases secure.[30]

Still, I'm convinced that the greatest threat to voting rights is not the handiwork of any foreign foe. It is internal to us as Americans. It's the erosion of democracy that ensues when people allow themselves to become cynical about voting—when they let themselves believe that voting does not matter or that their vote won't count. That pernicious idea needs to be called out and challenged, not just by elder statesmen and stateswomen like me, but by everyone who cherishes democracy.

Both history and today's headlines warn Americans not to take voting for granted. As long as I'm able, I intend to sound that warning too.

Acknowledgments

I owe a great debt to the people of Minnesota. Writing this book has reminded me anew of the extraordinary support I received from Minnesotans at almost every stage of my life, especially while I served in elective office. As secretary of state for twenty-four years, I was received with great kindness and courtesy throughout this state as I sought to encourage participation in democracy. The voters of my state gave me a precious gift, the opportunity to advance the common good. Thank you, Minnesota.

• • •

A special thanks, too, goes to 2016 Democratic presidential nominee Hillary Rodham Clinton for writing this book's foreword. Clinton is someone I have known and admired for more than thirty years as our professional lives periodically intersected. Her stellar contributions to this nation predate her stint as first lady from 1993 through 2000, her service as a US senator from New York from 2001 through 2008, and her leadership of the US State Department as its secretary from 2009 through 2012. She is a warm and thoughtful person whose commitment to democracy runs deep. I was touched by her immediate affirmative reply when I asked her during her October 2019 book-tour stop in Minneapolis about contributing to this book. And I'm very grateful to Alana Petersen, the former chief of staff to two Minnesota US senators and Clinton's 2016 campaign advisor for Minnesota, for making the staff connections needed to deliver Clinton's essay on time. Alana is a good friend and an ever-ready source of sound advice.

• • •

This book's origin can be traced to many voices through many years. Family, friends, and ordinary Minnesotans have repeatedly approached me since I left office in 1998, asking me to tell my story and share my thoughts about voting in a book. I was warming to the idea in late 2018 when I learned that Lori Sturdevant would soon retire from the Star Tribune Editorial Board after a forty-three-year career at the newspaper. Lori and I became well acquainted when she was the Minneapolis newspaper's lead reporter covering my US Senate campaign in 1984. I knew I would need a writing partner to produce a book. That's a role Lori has played with a number of other Minnesota political leaders, including former governor Elmer L. Andersen, civil rights leader W. Harry Davis, feminist leader Arvonne Fraser, and former US senator David Durenberger. I was delighted when she agreed to work with me.

The final push we needed came from Josh Leventhal, the director of the Minnesota Historical Society Press. He approached Lori in early 2019 in search of a fitting new title his publishing house could release in 2020 in connection with the one hundredth anniversary of women's suffrage. Lori and I agreed that if we got busy, we could fill that bill. We are grateful for the confidence, financial support, and expert guidance we received from Josh and his very professional crew at MNHS Press, including editor in chief Ann Regan, managing editor Shannon Pennefeather, and publicity manager Alison Aten. I'm also glad to have come to know exhibits researcher Ami Naff, who helped me mine the Minnesota History Center archives for this project.

We were honored by the affirmative responses that met us when we sought help from people who had been part of my story. Invaluable assistance came from Joe Mansky, who retired in early 2019 as Ramsey County's elections manager, and Tom Durand, who left my office in 1991, then returned to the secretary of state's office during Mark Ritchie's tenure. Gretchen Fogo shared her memories and archives from my 1972 legislative campaign and service in the Minnesota House. Ted Grindal recalled my state House term and 1984 Senate race. Bob Meek, Scott Benson, and Carole Faricy backstopped our memories of the 1984 race. So did Linda Holstein, one of the ten founders of Minnesota's Groweing. We were glad that another

Groweing founder, the late Barbara Stuhler, wrote a book about the experience. *No Regrets: Minnesota Women and the Joan Growe Senatorial Campaign,* published in 1986 by Braemar Press, provides a how-to manual for grassroots campaigning that remains relevant today. My cousin David Sadler supplied family history notes I lacked. Chief US District Court Judge John Tunheim helped us recall the early 1990s, when he served in the Minnesota attorney general's office.

For up-to-the-minute information on threats to ballot access today, we relied on Minnesota Secretary of State Steve Simon and his aide Peter Bartz-Gallagher, and Emma Greenman of the Center for Popular Democracy, a national network of statewide organizations with three staffers based in Minnesota. I'm pleased that Emma is making a bid for election to the legislature in 2020; I'll be cheering her on. For national data, we turned to the Brennan Center for Justice at New York University and the National Conference of State Legislatures, both respected sources of information about voting rights and trends.

It's fitting that the person who helped this project the most is also the one who was in my corner the longest: my mother, Lucille Mary Brown Anderson Johnson, whom everybody called Brownie. Mom remarried four years after Dad died; she died herself sixteen years later, in 2006. Among her legacies to me are about two dozen scrapbooks and photo albums that meticulously chronicle my entire twenty-six-year public career. Those big books shuttled back and forth between Lori's home office and mine as we scoured them for useful bits of history. Lori has said Brownie was so instrumental to this book's production that she deserves billing on its cover.

As we worked, I often wished I could consult with my longtime office partner and good friend, former deputy secretary of state Elaine Voss. For sixteen years, she was the anchor for our operation and a key participant in every decision we made. No elected official could have asked for a better chief aide. Alas, by 2019 she was living with dementia and other ailments. The sad word of her death came on December 21, 2019, as we were putting the final touches on chapters to which she surely would have contributed, had she been able. I will always be in her debt.

I can't think of Elaine without also remembering with gratitude the dedicated work of my secretary Jeanne McGree and administrative assistant Rich Pietz. They were key components in a team that served Minnesota democracy very well indeed.

Lori and I both owe abiding gratitude to our families. My children have scattered far but remain dear. My eldest son Michael and his wife Sally now live in Florida; daughter Colleen and her husband Julian live in New York; David and his family live in Draper, Utah; and Patrick lives in the Twin Cities. Lori's husband Martin Vos is an electrical engineer by profession, but he is also a multilingual grammarian whose voluntary editing clarified our message. My partner Tom Moore has been my sounding board, computer coach, and personal care-and-feeding aide as I've discovered all that is entailed in writing a book. His stalwart support has made a huge positive difference for me and for this project—hence this book's dedication to him.

My three granddaughters also share in this book's dedication. My hope for them and their generation is that they will forever keep and enjoy the blessings of a vigorous and genuinely inclusive American democracy.

Notes

Notes to Chapter 1: Rooted in Democracy

1. Chip Jones, "The Ten Largest Lakes in Minnesota," Minnesota Fun Facts, https://www.minnesotafunfacts.com/minnesota-geography/the-ten -largest-lakes-in-minnesota/.
2. A consensus-based version of village-level democracy was practiced in the land that became Minnesota long before Europeans and Americans arrived. For a description of Dakota and Ojibwe governing practices, see Lori Sturdevant, "Politics in Minnesota," MNopedia, Minnesota Historical Society, http://www.mnopedia.org/politics-minnesota.
3. Minneapolis Public Library staff, "A History of Minneapolis: Early History," https://web.archive.org/web/20070420010726/http://www.mpls .lib.mn.us/history/eh4.asp.
4. Daniel J. Elazar first described America's three political subcultures— individualistic, traditional, and moralistic—in his *American Federalism: A View from the States* (New York: Crowell, 1966) ("politics is ideally," 97). He elaborated on his conclusion that "Minnesota is the archetypical example of a state informed and permeated by a moralistic political subculture" in Daniel J. Elazar, Virginia Gray, and Wyman Spano, *Minnesota Politics and Government* (Lincoln: University of Nebraska Press, 1999), xxiv. Minnesota's moralism had practical limits, however. In 1849, its territorial legislature declared that "all persons [men] of a mixture of white and Indian blood and who shall have adopted the habits and customs of civilized men, are hereby declared to be entitled to all the rights and privileges" of voting. Extending the vote to those of mixed ancestry boosted population numbers so the territory could more quickly become a state: see Bruce M. White, "The Power of Whiteness, or, The Life and Times of Joseph Rolette Jr.," *Minnesota History* 56 (Winter 1998–99): 190. For a discussion of efforts to restrict these voters

and to bar African Americans from voting, see Mary Lethert Wingerd, *North Country: The Making of Minnesota* (Minneapolis: University of Minnesota Press, 2010), 225–27, 253, 389n75.

5. "Minnesota Now, Then, When: An Overview of Demographic Change," Minnesota State Demographic Center, April 2015. Colin Woodard made the argument about dominant political cultures in *American Nations: A History of the Eleven Rival Regional Cultures of North America* (New York: Penguin Books, 2011), relying in part on the work of Penn State University cultural geographer Wilbur Zelinsky.

6. Great-grandpa Charlie Brown was originally from a farm near Calais, Maine, close to the Canadian border. During his youth, his family moved in 1868 to an abandoned homestead near Sleepy Eye, Minnesota. Lured by good wages, Charlie left the farm in the mid-1870s to join a lumber camp near what would become Turtle Lake, Wisconsin. While there, he met Ellen Rosenbush, the daughter of a German immigrant who had come to the United States in time to serve in the Union Army in the Civil War. Charlie and Ellen were married in 1877 and raised a large family in Wisconsin.

7. More about Northern Pump Company and founder John B. Hawley is available in the Northern Pump Company Papers at the Minnesota History Center Library, St. Paul.

8. For more about the Gamble-Skogomo stores, see https://en.wikipedia .org/wiki/Gamble-Skogmo#History. For a brief history of Buffalo, Minnesota, see https://en.wikipedia.org/wiki/Buffalo,_Minnesota#History.

9. For a list of women in the Minnesota Legislature, see the Minnesota Legislative Reference Library (hereafter, MLRL): https://www.leg.state .mn.us/lrl/history/wmnpuboffterm.

10. That school is today's St. Cloud State University. The word *Teachers* was dropped from its name in 1957. For more on the school's history, see https://www.stcloudstate.edu/studenthandbook/history-traditions.aspx.

Notes to Chapter 2: What's a Government For?

1. Oliver C. Carmichael, "The Roots of Higher Education in Minnesota," *Minnesota History* 34, no. 3 (Summer 1954): 90–95. For the history of Marquette University, see https://www.marquette.edu/about/history .php.

2. A copy of the Northwest Ordinance of 1787 can be seen at www .ourdocuments.gov. Its importance to shaping the culture of the American Midwest is described by David G. McCullough in *Pioneers: The*

Heroic Story of the Settlers Who Brought the American Ideal West (New York: Simon and Schuster, 2019).

3. Minnesota had 336 school districts in 2019: see "List of School Districts in Minnesota," Ballotpedia, https://ballotpedia.org/List_of_school_districts_in_Minnesota. For an account of early legislative decisions concerning public education, see Minnesota State Department of Education, "A History of the State Department of Education in Minnesota," https://mn.gov/mnddc/past/pdf/60s/67/67-AHO-MDE.pdf.

4. Article XIII, Section 1, Minnesota Constitution. Kathleen A. Gaylord and Susan Chianelli Jacobson, "History of Taxation in Minnesota," Tax Study Commission, 1979, 26, https://www.leg.state.mn.us/docs/pre2003/other/792892.pdf.

5. Randy Furst, "Polly Mann Is Still Taking on War and Racism at Age 96," *Minneapolis Star Tribune*, February 25, 2016.

6. Minnesota Department of Human Services, "Welfare in Minnesota: Facts and Figures," February 2007, https://mn.gov/law-library-stat/archive/urlarchive/a060804.pdf.

Notes to Chapter 3: Riding the Second Wave

1. *The Feminine Mystique* by Betty Friedan (New York: W. W. Norton, 1963) was a best-selling book credited with sparking the beginning of the revived feminist movement of the 1960s and 1970s. It described the dissatisfaction of America's housewives with their lack of opportunity for meaningful work outside the home.

2. "Carrie Chapman Catt," History.com; Washington State Historical Society, "National Council of Women Voters"; League of Women Voters of the US, "100 Years of LWV."

3. About the special session of the Minnesota Legislature in September 1919, see https://www.leg.state.mn.us/lrl/history/spsess. League of Women Voters of Minnesota, "Our History." About the feminist movements in the twentieth century in Minnesota, see Lori Sturdevant, *Her Honor: Rosalie Wahl and the Minnesota Women's Movement* (St. Paul: Minnesota Historical Society Press, 2014).

4. Lois A. Glewwe, ed., *South St. Paul Centennial, 1887–1987: The History of South St. Paul, Minnesota* (South St. Paul, MN: Dakota County Historical Society, 1987), 239–42.

5. Ted Smebakken, "McCarthy Deals LBJ Camp Stiff Setback," *Minneapolis Star*, March 6, 1968, 1A.

6. For a contemporary analysis of McCarthy's role in Humphrey's defeat,

see Mary McGrory, "McCarthy Will Be Blamed if HHH Loses," *Minneapolis Tribune*, October 12, 1968, 4A.

7. Esther Wattenberg, "Women in the DFL . . . A Preliminary Report: Present but Powerless?" commissioned by the DFL Women's Caucus, May 1971, Koryne Horbal papers, 1962–2005, Minnesota History Center Library, St. Paul.

8. "In House Dist. 40, All Candidates Death on Taxes," *Minneapolis Star*, October 26, 1972, 13B.

9. For an account of those women twenty years after the Growe campaign, see Kay Miller, "Joan Growe's Political Legacy: Her 1972 Housewives' Campaign Proved Women Could Take the Heat Outside the Kitchen," *Minneapolis Star Tribune* Sunday Magazine, January 3, 1993, 4SM.

Notes to Chapter 4: Open Government

1. "Record 6 Women Win Seats in Legislature," *Minneapolis Star*, November 8, 1972, 17A. A roster of women elected to the legislature over time can be found at MLRL, https://www.leg.state.mn.us/lrl/history/women.

2. Peter Vaughan, "She Discovers House Chamber a Men's Room," *Minneapolis Star*, February 8, 1973, 15B.

3. For more information about the Equal Rights Amendment's ratification, see https://www.equalrightsamendment.org/.

4. Catalyst, "Women in the Workforce—United States: Quick Take," https://www.catalyst.org/research/women-in-the-workforce-united -states/. Joan Growe's personal files include a transcript of her January 22, 1973, House floor speech.

5. The amendment to "allow flexible legislative sessions" was approved with 54 percent of the vote: "State Constitutional Amendments Considered," MLRL, https://www.leg.state.mn.us/lrl/mngov/constitutional amendments.

6. Party control of the Minnesota Legislature from 1951 to the present is available at MLRL, https://www.leg.state.mn.us/lrl/history/.

7. Tom Berg, *Minnesota's Miracle: Learning from the Government that Worked* (Minneapolis: University of Minnesota Press, 2012), 59–77.

8. "Lindstrom: Campaign Funds Being Diverted," *Minneapolis Tribune*, April 15, 1972, 5A; Berg, *Minnesota's Miracle*, 26–28.

9. "Text of Governor's Message to Legislature," *Minneapolis Tribune*, January 4, 1973, 4–5A.

10. Minnesota Session Laws of 1957, chapter 773, H.F. 1718, https://www .revisor.mn.gov/laws/1957/0/Session+Law/Chapter/773/pdf/.

11. Dennis Cassano, "30 Volunteers Assist New Legislator," *Minneapolis Tribune*, March 21, 1973, 1A.

12. Berg, *Minnesota's Miracle*, 80–81. For the lasting impact of the open meeting requirements on the legislature, see Lori Sturdevant, "A New Kind of Chaos Takes Hold at the Capitol," *Minneapolis Star Tribune*, November 21, 2014.

13. "Senate Passes Open Meeting Bill," *Minneapolis Tribune*, May 5, 1973, 8B; *St. Cloud Times*, "Open Meetings Bill Approved by House," May 19, 1973, 4. For a description of today's open meeting requirements in Minnesota, see https://www.house.leg.state.mn.us/hrd/pubs/openmtg.pdf.

14. A National Conference of State Legislatures briefing paper reports that states experience on average a five percent boost in turnout with same-day registration: "Same Day Voter Registration," June 28, 2019, http://www.ncsl.org/research/elections-and-campaigns/same-day-registration.aspx.

15. Alexander Keyssar, *The Right to Vote: A Contested History of Democracy in the United States,* rev. ed. (New York: Basic Books, 2009), 99–101. John Seven, "The Exclusionary History of Voter Registration Dates to 1800," October 22, 2018, History.com. The literacy requirements sometimes also denied the vote to poor whites. Office of the North Dakota Secretary of State, "North Dakota, the Only State Without Voter Registration," August 2017. For information about the state's voter ID requirement, see Secretary of State, North Dakota: vip.sos.nd.gov.

16. Minnesota Session Laws for 1959, Chapter 675, Article II, https://www.revisor.mn.gov/laws/1959/0/Session+Law/Chapter/675/pdf/.

17. "Text of Governor's Message to Legislature" (1973). Voter turnout in Minnesota is available from the Minnesota Secretary of State's office, "Minnesota Election Statistics, 1950–2018": https://www.sos.state.mn.us/media/3609/minnesota-election-statistics-1950-to-2018.pdf.

18. General Laws of Minnesota for 1868, Chapter CVI, page 149. A description of the amendments to the Minnesota Constitution and the votes cast to adopt or reject them can be found at "State Constitutional Amendments Considered," MLRL.

19. A WalletHub study published February 17, 2016, shows that both states, however, ranked low in measures of black engagement in recent elections: Maine ranked forty-fourth in percentage of black voter registration in 2012, and Minnesota ranked forty-fifth in percentage of black voter turnout in the 2014 midterm election. For the latest rankings, see Richie Bernardo, "2020's States with the Highest Political Engagement

Among Blacks," https://wallethub.com/edu/where-are-blacks-most-least-politically-engaged/19026/#red-vs-blue.

20. Robert Franklin, "State League of Women Voters Endorses Voter-Registration Bill," *Minneapolis Tribune*, May 16, 1973, 2B.

21. Robert Franklin, "Senators Approved Election Day Registration," *Minneapolis Tribune*, May 11, 1973, 1B.

22. Editorial, "Easier Voter Registration," *Minneapolis Tribune*, May 18, 1973, 6A; Minnesota Secretary of State, "Minnesota Election Statistics, 1950–2018."

23. Glenn Adams, "History of 'Same-Day' Voter Registration in Maine," *Bangor Daily News*, November 5, 2011; "Registration Plan Sent to Anderson," *Minneapolis Tribune*, May 18, 1973, 2B; "Senators Approved Election-Day Registration," *Minneapolis Tribune*, May 11, 1973, 1B; Minnesota House Journal, Senate File 1246, 4230.

24. "Erdahl Asks Veto of Vote Bill," *Minneapolis Star*, May 18, 1973, 16B.

Notes to Chapter 5: Chief Election Officer

1. For more about the Young Turks in the Minnesota Legislature, see David Durenberger with Lori Sturdevant, *When Republicans Were Progressive* (St. Paul: Minnesota Historical Society Press, 2018), 56–63.

2. "Rep. Nelsen Will Not Seek His Ninth Term," *St. Cloud Daily Times*, December 28, 1973, 5A; Dave Hoium, "Loehr Eyes Erdahl Post," *St. Cloud Daily Times*, December 28, 1973, 1A.

3. The amendment making the term change was approved by voters in the 1958 election: "State Constitutional Amendments Considered," MLRL. Sturdevant, *Her Honor*, 86–87.

4. "Minnesota Secretary of State," Wikipedia.

5. "Compensation of Minnesota Legislators, 1858–Present," MLRL, https://www.leg.state.mn.us/lrl/history/salary.

6. Judith A. Center, "1972 Democratic Convention Reforms and Party Democracy," *Political Science Quarterly* 89, no. 2 (1974): 325–50.

7. Associated Press, "Congressional Hopeful Would Welcome Campaign Help from Nixon," *Bemidji Pioneer*, April 30, 1974, 3.

8. "Easy Endorsements Expected at DFL's State Convention," *Minneapolis Star*, June 13, 1974, 9A; Bernie Shellum, "DFL Chooses Joan Growe for State Post," *Minneapolis Tribune*, June 16, 1974, 1A.

9. "Returns of the Primary Election in State of Minnesota, September 15, 1970, for Representative in Congress," https://www.leg.state.mn.us/archive/sessions/electionresults/1970-09-15-p-man.pdf.

10. "State of Minnesota Primary Election, September 10, 1974, Vote Totals," https://www.leg.state.mn.us/archive/sessions/electionresults/1974-09 -10-p-sec.pdf; Joe Blade, "DFL's Auditor Choice Falls Hard; Growe Is Secretary of State Pick," *Minneapolis Star*, September 11, 1974, 16B.

11. Gerry Nelson, "Secretary of State Race Unique on State Ballot," *Rochester Post-Bulletin*, October 4, 1974, 11.

12. Steven Dornfeld, "Growe Asks Vote for Ability, not Her Sex," *Minneapolis Tribune*, October 18, 1974, 1B; Growe's personal files.

13. "Joan Growe Seeks State Ombudsman," *Red Wing Republican Eagle*, October 21, 1974; "Growe Proposes Minnesota Ombudsman," *Bemidji Pioneer*, October 21, 1974; "Grow Proposes Ombudsman Post," *Marshall Messenger Independent*, October 21, 1974.

14. "Poll: Anderson Leads, Growe Passes Erdahl," *Minneapolis Tribune*, November 4, 1974, 1A.

15. Bernie Shellum, "GOP Hurt Most by Lack of Republicans at the Polls," *Minneapolis Tribune*, November 6, 1974, 1A.

Notes to Chapter 6: The Traveling Secretary

1. Forrest Talbott memo, December 15, 1970, Joan Growe papers, 1973–1998, box 101.H.5.4F, Minnesota History Center Library, St. Paul.

2. Minnesota Secretary of State's Office, "Become an Election Judge," https://www.sos.state.mn.us/elections-voting/get-involved/become-an -election-judge/#who-can-apply.

3. Mary Ann McCoy obituary, *Minneapolis Star Tribune*, October 24, 2010. See also Prabook, "Mary Ann McCoy," https://prabook.com/web/ mary_ann.mccoy/509532.

4. Minnesota Secretary of State, "Minnesota Election Statistics, 1950–2018."

5. Joan Growe papers, box 101.H.5.4F.

6. A 1976 meeting in southeastern Minnesota is described in Terry Bormann, "Election Laws, Training Detailed," *Winona Daily News*, April 30, 1976, 3.

7. Betty Wilson, "State Secretary's Office Criticized on Cash Handling," *Minneapolis Star*, July 24, 1975; Joan Growe papers, box 101.H.5.5B.

8. "Mrs. Growe Asks Inquiry on *Star* Story," *Minneapolis Star*, July 26, 1975, 9A.

9. "Higher Voting Percentages Sought in State," *St. Cloud Times*, September 2, 1976, 24; Harley Sorenson, "St. Paul Challenges City to Vote Contest," *Minneapolis Tribune*, October 20, 1976, 2B.

10. Editorial, "Voters' Record Turnout," *Minneapolis Tribune*, November 19,

1976, 10A; Minnesota Secretary of State, "Minnesota Election Statistics, 1950–2018"; Associated Press, "Minnesota Voter Turnout Leads the Nation," *Fergus Falls Daily Journal*, November 16, 1976, 1.

11. Dr. Gerald Brekke obituary, http://www.genealogybuff.com/nd/state/webbbs_config.pl/noframes/read/134.

12. "Brekke Suggests Perforated Ballots," *St. Cloud Daily Times*, September 30, 1978, 13; "Brekke Criticizes Same-Day Registration," *St. Cloud Daily Times*, October 14, 1978, 22.

13. Minnesota Secretary of State's Office, "Register on Election Day," https://www.sos.state.mn.us/elections-voting/register-to-vote/register-on-election-day/; Joe Mansky email with Sturdevant, January 8, 2020; Natasha Khan and Corbin Carson, "Cases of Voter-ID Election Fraud Found 'Virtually Non-Existent,'" MinnPost, August 13, 2012.

14. Editorial, "Six Other Statewide Races," *Minneapolis Tribune*, October 31, 1978, 6A.

15. "Minnesota Election Results 1978: Primary Election and General Election," https://www.leg.state.mn.us/archive/sessions/electionresults/1978-11-07-g-sec.pdf.

16. Steven Dornfeld, "The Hows and Whys of Minnesota's Vote," *Minneapolis Tribune*, November 9, 1978, 14A. All three of the DFLers Rasmussen mentioned would try for higher office in the 1980s. None would succeed.

17. Sturdevant, *Her Honor*, ch. 5.

18. Lori Sturdevant, "Women's Meeting Vote Backs Right to Terminate Pregnancy," *Minneapolis Tribune*, June 5, 1977, 1A.

19. "Morrison County DFL Leadership Calls for Joan Growe to Resign," *Minneapolis Tribune*, June 23, 1977, 5B; "Winona County DFL Backs Mrs. Growe," *Winona Daily News*, July 15, 1977, 12.

20. Betty Wilson, "House Split Is Putting Growe in the Limelight," *Minneapolis Star*, December 22, 1978, 1.

21. Associated Press, "Pavlak Eligible for Reelection," *St. Cloud Times*, May 26, 1979, 3.

22. An example of the kind of coverage my travels generated: "Growe May Seek New Heights," *Winona Daily News*, October 31, 1981, 1A.

23. Associated Press, "Growe Joins Movement to Draft Kennedy," *Minneapolis Tribune*, September 26, 1979, 2B.

24. Associated Press, "Spannaus Choice Upsets Women," *St. Cloud Daily Times*, May 26, 1982, 2.

25. In the late 1960s, at Horbal's urging, the state DFL party changed the names of its leaders to "chair" and "associate chair."

Notes to Chapter 7: Running "As a Woman"

1. The newspaper's name changed twice in the 1980s.
2. Steve Berg, "Growe Explores Bid Against Boschwitz in Washington Trip," *Minneapolis Star Tribune*, July 29, 1983, 3B.
3. Center for the American Woman and Politics, "The Gender Gap: Voting Choices in Presidential Elections," Rutgers University, New Brunswick, NJ, 2017, http://www.cawp.rutgers.edu/sites/default/files/resources/ggpresvote.pdf.
4. Betty Wilson, "Growe Announces for Senate," *Minneapolis Star Tribune*, October 3, 1983, 3B.
5. See Durenberger with Sturdevant, *When Republicans Were Progressive*.
6. Paul Levy, "Women in Government: There Are More, but State Majority Remains Tiny Minority in Officialdom," *Minneapolis Star Tribune*, January 24, 1983, 3B.
7. Lori Sturdevant, "Boschwitz Has Funds but No Foes, for Now," *Minneapolis Star Tribune*, June 8, 1983, 1A.
8. Lori Sturdevant, "Boschwitz Financially Ahead of Challengers," *Minneapolis Star Tribune*, February 1, 1984, 1A; Associated Press, "Boschwitz Leads Fundraisers," *Winona Daily News*, April 17, 1984, 11; Lori Sturdevant, "Joan Growe's First-Ballot Lead Edges Upwards," *Minneapolis Star Tribune*, June 15, 1984, 1B.
9. Lori Sturdevant, "Life Toughened Growe for Senate Race," *Minneapolis Star Tribune*, June 3, 1983, 1A.
10. Lori Sturdevant, "Oberstar Attacks Growe on Abortion," *Minneapolis Star Tribune*, June 11, 1984, 1B.
11. "Where the Senate Candidates Stand," *Minneapolis Tribune*, April 1, 1984, 6A.
12. Lori Sturdevant, "Growe Wins DFL Endorsement," *Minneapolis Star Tribune*, June 18, 1984, 1A.
13. David Phelps and Lori Sturdevant, "4 DFL Congressmen Urge Support for Growe," *Minneapolis Star Tribune*, June 22, 1984, 3B; Associated Press, "Oberstar Ends Senate Bid, Will Run for House," *St. Cloud Times*, June 25, 1984, 18; Associated Press, "Anderson Quits Race," *Winona Daily News*, July 6, 1984, 9.
14. Sturdevant, *Her Honor*, 137–42.
15. Betty Wilson, "Officials Say Mattson Holds Office, Seldom Occupies It," *Minneapolis Star Tribune*, June 8, 1983, 1A.
16. Barbara Stuhler, *No Regrets: Minnesota Women and the Joan Growe Senatorial Campaign* (St. Paul, MN: Braemar Press, 1986).

17. Lori Sturdevant, "Growe-Mattson Primary Race Fireworks Haven't Ignited," *Minneapolis Star Tribune*, September 8, 1984, 1A.

18. Lori Sturdevant, "Boschwitz Leads Growe by 21 Points," *Minneapolis Star Tribune*, August 17, 1984, 1A.

19. Lori Sturdevant, "Mondale-Reagan Race Too Close to Call," *Minneapolis Star Tribune*, August 19, 1984, 1A.

20. Frank Newport, Jeffrey M. Jones, and Lydia Saad, "Ronald Reagan from the People's Perspective: A Gallup Poll Review," Gallup News Service, June 7, 2004; Ellen Goodman, "Joan Growe's Uphill Struggle," *Minneapolis Star Tribune*, October 30, 1984, 14.

21. Lori Sturdevant, "DFL Worries about Catching Boschwitz," *Minneapolis Star Tribune*, March 25, 1984, 1A; Associated Press, "Growe, Boschwitz Report Donations, Campaign Spending," *St. Cloud Times*, October 16, 1984, 18. DFL candidate Mark Dayton had spent more than $7 million in 1982, but his campaign was largely self-financed.

22. Betty Wilson, "Thousands Greet Ferraro," *Minneapolis Star Tribune*, September 20, 1984, 1A.

23. Lori Sturdevant, "Growe TV Ad Assails Boschwitz on Taxes," *Minneapolis Star Tribune*, September 29, 1984.

24. Lori Sturdevant, "Boschwitz Leads Growe by Only 10 Percentage Points," *Minneapolis Star Tribune*, October 19, 1984, 1A; Wes Volkenant, "Growe's Commercials," *Minneapolis Star Tribune*, October 2, 1984, 7A; Maureen Dowd, "Harsh Assertions Mark Minnesota's Senate Race," *New York Times*, October 29, 1984, 19A.

25. "Mrs. Growe, You've Gone Too Far," advertisement paid for by People for Boschwitz, *Minneapolis Star Tribune*, October 23, 1984, 14B.

26. "Poll: Two-Thirds of Voters Think Trump Should Release His Tax Returns," The Hill.com, February 21, 2018.

27. Anna Dickie Olesen was the Democratic Party nominee for the US Senate in Minnesota in 1922. She was the first woman in the nation to win major-party nomination for the Senate. She came in third with 17 percent of the vote, behind the Farmer-Labor Party winner, Henrik Shipstead, and Republican Frank B. Kellogg. "1922 United States Senate Election in Minnesota," Wikipedia.

Notes to Chapter 8: Modernizing Democracy

1. Jacqui Banaszynski, "Growe Is Winner in Women's Cause," *St. Paul Pioneer Press*, November 8, 1984, 3A.

2. Speech in Growe's personal files.

3. "About Us: Ellen R. Malcolm," Emily's List, https://www.emilyslist.org/bios/entry/ellen-malcolm.

4. Tad Vezner, "He's the Go-To Person about State Elections Policy. Now Joe Mansky Is Retiring," *St. Paul Pioneer Press*, March 2, 2019.

5. "Hokr, Dorothy I.," MLRL, https://www.leg.state.mn.us/legdb/fulldetail?ID=10261.

6. Betty Wilson, "Carlson to Decide on Write-In Effort Today," *Minneapolis Star Tribune*, September 18, 1990, 1A.

7. "Legislative Election Recounts," MLRL, https://www.leg.state.mn.us/legdb/elections?type=recount.

8. Gregor Pinney, "Splitting Ballots Canceled 68,000 Votes in Primary," *Minneapolis Star Tribune*, September 24, 1986, 6B.

9. George Deukmejian bested Democrat Tom Bradley among absentee voters by more than 113,000 votes: Cathleen Decker, "Maybe Race Wasn't the Only Factor," *Los Angeles Times*, October 29, 2008. Not until 2006, when Republicans controlled the state House, did the legislature restrict the number of nonregistered voters for whom one person could sign registration vouchers: Office of the Revisor of Statutes, Minnesota Session Laws—2006, Regular Session, chapter 242, https://www.revisor.mn.gov/laws/2006/0/242/.

10. Editorial, "Mail Election Gives More Voice to Voters," *St. Cloud Daily Times*, September 3, 1987, 4A; Office of the Minnesota Secretary of State, "2018 Mail Voting Guide," https://www.sos.state.mn.us/media/3064/mail-voting-guide.pdf.

11. Rachel Stassen-Berger, "No Excuse Needed to Vote Absentee in Minnesota," *Minneapolis Star Tribune*, June 23, 2014.

12. William Claiborne, "Democrat Wins Oregon Senate Race," *Washington Post*, January 31, 1996.

13. Office of the Revisor of Statutes, Minnesota Session Laws—1987, Regular Session, chapter 361, https://www.revisor.mn.gov/laws/1987/0/361/.

14. Dane Smith, "Growe Fears Voters Will Stay Away in Droves," *Minneapolis Star Tribune*, November 3, 1988, 7B.

15. "Computers: System to Expand Access to State Data," *Minneapolis Star Tribune*, February 15, 1988.

16. Betty Wilson and David Phelps, "Caucus Deal with National Party Is at Risk, DFL Says," *Minneapolis Star Tribune*, December 3, 1987, 1B; Betty Wilson, "DFL, National Party Settle Caucus Dispute," February 11, 1988, 1A.

17. "Heavy Load of Caucus Results Poured in Smoothly, Despite a Few Minor Glitches," *Minneapolis Star Tribune*, February 24, 1988, 8A; editorial

praise for Growe included the *St. Paul Pioneer Press*, "All Minnesotans Won in Caucuses Tuesday," and the *Minneapolis Star Tribune*, "And the Caucus Winners Were . . . ," both published February 25, 1988.

18. Joe Mansky interview with the authors, xxxadd date.

19. Dan Oberdorfer, "Turnout in State Falls; About 65% of Those Eligible to Vote," *Minneapolis Star Tribune*, November 10, 1988, 21A.

20. "Politician Wants to Be Last Secretary of State," *Pipestone County Star*, October 7, 1982.

21. Jim Klobuchar, "Nothing Can Scare Joan Growe Now," *Minneapolis Star Tribune*, June 9, 1985, 1B; Lori Sturdevant, "Bill Would Let Voters Combine 3 Offices," *Minneapolis Star Tribune*, March 26, 1985, 1B.

22. "Minnesota Election Results 1990: Primary Election and General Election," MLRL, https://www.leg.state.mn.us/archive/sessions/electionresults/1990-09-11-p-sec.pdf.

23. Allen Short, "Allegations Rock Governor's Race," *Minneapolis Star Tribune*, October 15, 1990, 1A.

24. "IR: Top Leaders Ponder Possible Alternatives," *Minneapolis Star Tribune*, October 18, 1990, 16A.

25. Betty Wilson, Dane Smith, and Randy Furst, "Write-In Bid Begun by Auditor," *Minneapolis Star Tribune*, October 23, 1990, 1A.

26. Allen Short and Paul McEnroe, "When Did Grunseth 'Wild Years' End?" *Minneapolis Star Tribune*, October 28, 1990, 1A.

27. Betty Wilson, "Clark-or-Dyrstad Decision in Hands of Supreme Court," *Minneapolis Star Tribune*, November 1, 1990, 1B.

28. Robert Whereatt, "IR Team Is Carlson-Dyrstad," *Minneapolis Star Tribune*, November 2, 1990, 1A; email to author from John R. Tunheim, chief judge of the US District Court for Minnesota, January 24, 2020.

29. "The Governor's Race/Three Scenarios," *Minneapolis Star Tribune*, October 2, 1990, 1A.

30. Monica M. Manning, "Growe's Integrity" (letters from readers), *Minneapolis Star Tribune*, November 16, 1990.

Notes to Chapter 9: The Nation's Leader

1. US Census Bureau, Historical Reported Voting Rates, https://www.census.gov/data/tables/time-series/demo/voting-and-registration/voting-historical-time-series.html.

2. Bureau of the Census Statistical Brief, "The Decline in American Voter Turnout," November 1991, https://www.census.gov/population/socdemo/voting/SB91-23.pdf. Five Minnesota secretaries of state have been Na-

tional Association of Secretaries of State presidents: Mike Holm, Joseph Donovan, Joan Anderson Growe, Mary Kiffmeyer, and Mark Ritchie: https://www.nass.org/sites/default/files/nass-history/5-Presidents-19.pdf.

3. "What the End of Ohio's Golden Week Means for Minority Voters," *Pacific Standard*, September 16, 2016.

4. Matthew Hutchison, "Durenberger, Four Others Blocking 'Motor Voter' Bill," *Minneapolis Star Tribune*, March 16, 1993, 7; "National Motor Voter Bill Signed," *Minnesota Ballot Bulletin* 4, no. 2 (July 1993).

5. National Democratic Institute: www.ndi.org. Growe's other missions as an election observer were in Romania in 1992, South Africa in 1994, Azerbaijan in 1998, El Salvador in 1999, and Peru in 2001.

6. Marc Lallanilla, "5 Intriguing Facts about the Roma," Live Science, October 23, 2013, https://www.livescience.com/40652-facts-about-roma-romani-gypsies.html; "Evolution in Europe; Romanian Election Is Valid Despite Flaws, US Declares," *New York Times*, May 26, 1990.

7. Pat Deninger, "Growe Calls for High Voter Turnout," *Winona Daily News*, August 21, 1990, 5A.

8. Lisa Grace Lednicer, "Minnesota Observers Find Election Thrilling," *St. Paul Pioneer Press*, April 29, 1994.

9. Lee Rood, "South Africa's Election Should Be Lesson for Minnesota, Growe Says," *St. Cloud Times*, May 11, 1994, 1A.

10. Betty Wilson, "Voting Overhaul," *Minneapolis Star Tribune*, January 27, 1991, 1B.

11. Joan Anderson Growe, "Voting by Mail Can Boost Turnout, Cut Per-Vote Election Costs, Growe Says," *Minnesota Journal*, April 9, 1991.

12. Dennis J. McGrath, "Growe Envisions a Mail-In Primary," *Minneapolis Star Tribune*, May 16, 1991, 1B.

13. Dane Smith, "Like It or Not, Parties Will Feel Effects of Primary," *Minneapolis Star Tribune*, January 18, 1992; Editorial, "Go for the Presidential Primary by Mail," *Minneapolis Star Tribune*, January 12, 1992, 19A; Dane Smith, "Carlson Elects to Have Primary," *Minneapolis Star Tribune*, January 17, 1992, 1A.

14. "Vetoes Summary," MLRL, https://www.leg.state.mn.us/lrl/vetoes/vetogov.

15. Details of the fourteen bills and the timing of the governor's actions are spelled out in *Senate v. Carlson*, C3–91–7547, Ramsey County District Court, August 2, 1991, https://www.leg.state.mn.us/webcontent/lrl/guides/Redistricting/Senate_v_Carlson_1991-08-02_C3-91-7547.pdf.

16. The 1991–93 redistricting saga is told in "Redistricting 1990, a Minnesota Issues Resource Guide," MLRL, https://www.leg.state.mn.us/lrl/guides/ guides?issue=redistr. Charley Shaw, "Redistricting Has Been a Mess in Each of the Past Four Decades," *Minnesota Lawyer,* October 16, 2010.

17. Lawrence Lessig, *They Don't Represent Us: Reclaiming Our Democracy* (New York: Harper Collins, 2019), 19–30; "Redistricting Reform Report," January 11, 2008, Humphrey Institute of Public Affairs, https:// conservancy.umn.edu/bitstream/handle/11299/184709/Redistricting_ Reform_Report%20%281%29.pdf.

18. David Chanen, "Project Tries to Attract Young Voters," *Minneapolis Star Tribune,* June 1, 1992, 2B; Dane Smith, "Businesses Helping State Government Promote the Vote," *Minneapolis Star Tribune,* October 14, 1992, 2B; Bob von Sternberg, "More than 60,000 Have Registered as Part of Successful Voter Drive," *Minneapolis Star Tribune,* October 28, 1992.

19. US Census Bureau, Historical Reported Voting Rates.

20. Dane Smith, "Campaigns Put Best Face on Caucus Tally," *Minneapolis Star Tribune,* March 3, 1994, 1B.

21. Durenberger with Sturdevant, *When Republicans Were Progressive,* 222–23.

22. Editorial, "Fix Caucuses: Party Endorsement System Needs Reform," *Minneapolis Star Tribune,* March 13, 1994, 24A.

23. Members of the Growe Commission were state representative Ron Abrams, R-Minnetonka; Hy Berman, University of Minnesota history professor; Harriette Burkhalter of the Jefferson Center; Kay Erickson of the League of Women Voters; state senator Carol Flynn, DFL-Minneapolis; John French, attorney and DFL activist; Joan Higinbotham of Common Cause; state senator Sheila Kiscaden, R-Rochester (later DFL-Rochester); state representative Bernie Lieder, DFL-Crookston; Steve Sandell of the Humphrey Forum; former state representative Linda Scheid, DFL-Brooklyn Park (later a state senator); Charles Slocum, former state IR Party chair; Frank Sorauf, University of Minnesota political science professor; Marcea Staten, vice president and assistant general counsel, Medtronic Inc.; Roger Sween, Minnesota Study Circles Network; Claire Thoen-Levin, former state DFL Party chair; Stephen Young, attorney and Republican activist. The commission's report is available at https://www.leg.state.mn.us/docs/2005/other/050564.pdf.

24. Renee Richardson, "Growe Opponent Kimbler Knows He Faces Uphill Fight," *Brainerd Daily Dispatch,* July 11, 1994, 1A.

25. Editorial, "Voting Kids: Mock Elections Bill Deserved to Live," *Minneapolis Star Tribune*, May 20, 1994, 24A.

26. Editorial, "Reforms Can Save Much-Reviled System," *St. Paul Pioneer Press*, February 22, 1995; Editorial, "June Primary: Election Bill Has Other Good Features," *Minneapolis Star Tribune*, May 5, 1995, 22A; Editorial, "Undemocratic: Blame House for Lack of Election Reform," *Minneapolis Star Tribune*, May 28, 1995.

27. Associated Press, "State's Voter Turnout Was Record Low," *Minneapolis Star Tribune*, November 20, 1996, 4B.

28. Patricia Lopez Baden, "Six Terms Later, Growe Says It's Time to Quit," *Minneapolis Star Tribune*, September 12, 1997, 1A.

29. Lori Sturdevant, "Growe and the Office She Transformed," *Minneapolis Star Tribune*, October 30, 1998, 27A; Steven E. Schier, "No Fluke: Political Trends Fueled Ventura's Victory," *Minneapolis Star Tribune*, November 17, 1998, A15. See also Minnesota Secretary of State, "Canvassing Board Report, State General Election," November 3, 1998, https://official documents.sos.state.mn.us/Files/GetDocument/24001.

Notes to Chapter 10: How to Keep the State That Votes

1. Abdi Latif Dahir, "Trump's Existential Threat Has Fueled the Rise of Minnesota's Somali Political Class," *Quartz Africa*, November 6, 2018.

2. James Nord, "Rep. Kiffmeyer, Former Gov. Carlson Clash on Voting Amendment's Costs and Effects," MinnPost, October 10, 2012; Elizabeth Dunbar, "Rep. Sabo Offers Voter Registration Bill," *Minneapolis Star Tribune*, September 25, 2003, A18. For a list of studies of voter fraud, see Brennan Center, "Debunking the Voter Fraud Myth," January 31, 2017, https://www.brennancenter.org/our-work/research-reports/debunking-voter-fraud-myth. Sabo had been Speaker of the Minnesota House when Election Day registration was enacted in 1973.

3. Election Day registration increases turnout: see Barry C. Burden, David T. Canon, Kenneth R. Mayer, and Donald P. Moynihan, "The Effects and Costs of Early Voting, Election Day Registration, and Same Day Registration in the 2008 Elections," University of Wisconsin-Madison, report to the Pew Charitable Trusts, December 21, 2009, https://www.pewtrusts.org/~/media/legacy/uploadedfiles/pcs_assets/2009/uwisconsin1pdf.pdf. National Conference of State Legislatures, "Same-Day Voter Registration," June 28, 2019, http://www.ncsl.org/research/elections-and-campaigns/same-day-registration.aspx.

4. Cover story with photo featuring Governor Wendell Anderson and a fish: "The Good Life in Minnesota," *Time*, August 13, 1973.

5. Daniel Markovits and Ian Ayres, "The U.S. Is in a Perpetual State of Minority Rule," *Washington Post*, November 8, 2018.

6. Brennan Center for Justice, "How Minnesota's Photo ID Amendment Was Defeated," November 19, 2012, https://www.brennancenter.org/our-work/ analysis-opinion/how-minnesotas-voter-id-amendment-was-defeated.

7. Minnesota AFL-CIO, "'Our Vote Our Future' Statewide Campaign Launched to Defeat Photo ID Amendment," April 15, 2012, https://www .mnaflcio.org/updates/our-vote-our-future%E2%80%9D-statewide -campaign-launched-defeat-photo-id-amendment; Brennan Center for Justice, "Citizens Without Proof," November 2006, https://www.brennan center.org/sites/default/files/legacy/d/download_file_39242.pdf.

8. Joe Mansky's testimony is available at Senate Media Archives, 2012 Archive Video Collection, Committee Hearings, Thursday, March 1, 2012, Finance, minute 47: https://www.senate.mn/media/media_list.php? ls=87&ver=new&archive_year=2012&category=committee&type= video#header.

9. Office of the Minnesota Secretary of State, Results for Constitutional Amendments, November 6, 2012, https://electionresults.sos.state.mn.us/ Results/AmendmentResultsStatewide/1.

10. Danielle Root and Aadam Barclay, "Voter Suppression During the 2018 Midterm Elections," a paper produced for the Center for American Progress, November 20, 2018, https://www.americanprogress.org/issues/ democracy/reports/2018/11/20/461296/voter-suppression-2018-midterm -elections/.

11. Ari Berman, "How the 2000 Election in Florida Led to a New Wave of Voter Disenfranchisement," *The Nation*, July 28, 2015; Kevin Morris, Myrna Pérez, Jonathan Brater, and Christopher Deluzio, "Purges: A Growing Threat to the Right to Vote," Brennan Center for Justice, July 20, 2018, https://www.brennancenter.org/our-work/research-reports/ purges-growing-threat-right-vote.

12. P. R. Lockhart, "Georgia Put 53,000 Voter Registrations on Hold, Fueling New Charges of Voter Suppression," Vox.com, October 12, 2018; P. R. Lockhart, "Georgia, 2018's Most Prominent Voting Rights Battleground, Explained," Vox.com, November 6, 2018.

13. Fair Fight, www.fairfight.com.

14. Associated Press, "Georgia Moving Forward with Mass Voter Purge Monday," *New York Times*, December 19, 2019; Scott Bauer, "Judge: 234K

Wisconsin Voter Registrations Should Be Tossed," *Minneapolis Star Tribune*, December 13, 2019.

15. Rochelle Olson, "State Supreme Court Allows Voter Data Withheld from Public," *Minneapolis Star Tribune*, April 8, 2020.

16. Meghan McCann and Wendy Underhill, "Provisional Ballots," August 2015, National Conference of State Legislatures, http://www.ncsl.org/research/elections-and-campaigns/lb-provisional-ballots.aspx.

17. Mark Ritchie, "Swift Action Needed to Save Same-Day Registration," *Winona Daily News*, March 30, 2012, 6.

18. Brennan Center for Justice, "Automatic Voter Registration, a Summary," July 10, 2019, https://www.brennancenter.org/our-work/research-reports/automatic-voter-registration-summary. Governor Tim Pawlenty's veto letter is available at https://www.leg.state.mn.us/archive/vetoes/2009 veto_ch162.pdf.

19. Steve Simon, personal communication with the author.

20. ProCon.org, "Historical Timeline: US History of Felon Voting/Disenfranchisement," June 25, 2013, https://felonvoting.procon.org/historical-timeline/#1900-1949.

21. National Conference of State Legislatures, "Felon Voting Rights," October 14, 2019, http://www.ncsl.org/research/elections-and-campaigns/felon-voting-rights.aspx; Peter Callaghan, "Despite Concerns, Push to Cap Probation in Minnesota Moving Forward," MinnPost, December 16, 2019; Minnesota House of Representatives, Matt Gehring, "Election Crimes and Civil Penalties in Minnesota," information brief, July 2011, https://www.house.leg.state.mn.us/hrd/pubs/mnelectcrime.pdf.

22. Office of the Minnesota Secretary of State, "2018 Election Judge Guide," 2, https://www.sos.state.mn.us/media/2090/election-judge-guide.pdf.

23. National Conference of State Legislatures, "Preregistration for Young Voters," February 12, 2019, http://www.ncsl.org/research/elections-and-campaigns/preregistration-for-young-voters.aspx. For information about the civics test requirement, see the Minnesota Council for the Social Studies, "Civics Test in Minnesota Schools," http://www.mcss.org/Civics-Test.

24. Greta Kaul, "The University of Minnesota Has Some of the Highest Voter Turnout in the Country. It's Trying to Get It Even Higher," MinnPost, December 13, 2019.

25. Editorial, "Please Vote, Unless You Already Did," *Minneapolis Star Tribune*, November 2, 2018.

26. Jeff Hargarten, "637,581 People Voted Early in Minnesota. Here's What We Watched," *Minneapolis Star Tribune*, November 8, 2018.

27. Root and Barclay, "Voter Suppression During the 2018 Midterm Elections"; Colin Campbell, "Early Voting Reduced in 23 NC Counties; 9 Drop Sunday Voting After NCGOP Memo," *Raleigh News and Observer*, September 6, 2016.

28. "Native Americans Weren't Guaranteed the Right to Vote in Every State Until 1962," History.com, August 20, 2019.

29. Vann Newkirk II, "How *Shelby County v. Holder* Broke America," *The Atlantic*, July 10, 2018.

30. Sean Gallagher, "DHS, FBI Say Election Systems in All 50 States Were Targeted in 2016," ARS Technica, April 10, 2019. For an analysis of unfunded elections cybersecurity measures, see the Brennan Center, "Defending Elections: Federal Funding Needs for State Elections Security," a project of the Brennan Center for Justice, the University of Pittsburgh Institute for Cyber Law, Policy, and Security, R Street Institute, and the Alliance for Securing Democracy, July 18, 2019: https://www.brennancenter.org/sites/default/files/2019-08/Report_Defending_Elections.pdf.

Index

Page numbers in *italics* indicate illustrations.

straw poll of party caucus results, 127
vote, right to. *See* franchise
voter turnout: 1972 election, 51–52;
1974 election, 71–72; 1980
election, 85; 1984 DFL primary
election, 105, 106; 1984 election,
110; 1990 election, 133; 1992
election, 148–49; 1994, 154;
1994 precinct caucuses, 149;
1996 election, 154; 1998 election,
157; and age, 52; and automatic
registration, 144, 168–69, 171;
effect of high, on government
and political parties, 1–2, 159;
failure of Republican, in 1974
election, 68; and Fair Fight, 164;
and government-issued photo-
identification card requirement,
161–63; and high quality of
Minnesota life, 1–2; and Hopkins method of campaigning, 34;
in low-income neighborhoods,
159; and mail balloting, 123, 124;
Minnesota as US leader in, 5,
139; and "no-excuses" absentee
voting, 172; and party affiliation,
161; and polling stations on
college campuses, 172; and preregistration, 171; and same-day
voter registration, 79, 135, 137,
160, 185n14; typical primary
election, in Minnesota, 145; Vote
'76 campaign, 76, 77, 78
Voting Rights Act (1965), 52–53,
174

Wahl, Rosalie, 81, 102
Walz, Tim, 175
Wangen, Nancy, 36, 37, 42

Warsame, Abdi, 160
Washington Post, 124
Watergate, 57, 71–72, 73
Wattenberg, Esther, 33
WCCO, 17
Weinblatt, Alan, 132
Welch, Susie, 13
Welch, Thomas, 13
Wellstone, Paul, 133
Wemlinger, Sharon, 72
West, Jean, 104
Whitney, Wheelock, 90
Wilson, Betty, 103
Winkler, Mark, 41, 70–71
Wisconsin, 165
women: attitude toward working,
39; franchise for, 27–28; as just
housewives, 35; opportunities
for, during Growe's childhood
and teenage years, 15–16;
percent in workforce, 44–45;
as power behind male political campaigns, 37–38; voting
choices as different from men's,
89; voting first time in Minnesota, 27–29. *See also* feminists and feminism; League of
Women Voters
women in Minnesota Legislature:
1922–late 1960s, 15, 29; 1970,
34; 1972 number campaigning
for, 43; 1973 sworn in, 43; 1983,
92; 1997, 156; 2019, 156; Growe's
election to, 57; Growe's first
speech in House, 44–45
women in politics: allowed to run
for statewide office, 29; and
Anderson's openness in government agenda, 47–48; appointed
to complete husbands' unfinished

The text of *Turnout: Making Minnesota the State That Votes* was typeset in Warnock Pro, a serif typeface designed by Robert Slimbach. The typeface is named after John Warnock, one of the co-founders of Adobe and was released as a commercial font by Adobe in 2000.

Interior book design and layout by Wendy Holdman.